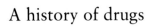

A history of drugs

Lydia Mez-Mangold

A history of drugs

Parthenon Publishing
THE PARTHENON PUBLISHING GROUP LIMITED

BARNES & NOBLE BOOKS
TOTOWA, NEW JERSEY

First published in the USA 1986 by
Barnes and Noble Books
81, Adams Drive
Totowa, New Jersey 07512

Library of Congress Cataloging-in-Publication Data

Mez-Mangold, Lydia.
    A history of drugs

    Bibliography: p.
    Includes index.
    1. Drugs – History.   I. Title.   [DNLM: 1. Drugs – history.
QV 11.1 M617h]
RS61.M49   1986   615'.1'09   86–10919
ISBN 0-389-20638-5

Published in the UK and Europe by:
The Parthenon Publishing Group Ltd
Casterton Hall
Carnforth, Lancs. UK

This edition is derived from an original colour production originated
by F. Hoffmann-La Roche & Co. Ltd., Basle, Switzerland.
© 1971 by F. Hoffman-La Roche & Co. Ltd., Basle, Switzerland.

Printed in Great Britain

Contents

Foreword

by Dr. phil. Alfons Lutz,
Honorary Lecturer in the
History of Pharmacy
at the University of Basle

From time immemorial mankind has adopted a fateful attitude towards disease and, in attempting to combat disease with drugs, men have interpreted the mysterious power of medicines either in material or magical terms, depending on the particular stage of human evolution.

The animism of earlier times sustained belief in a kind of spiritual matter pervading the universe. This substance was said to be present in different concentrations in inanimate objects and in living things. When this spiritual matter (it is tempting to try to equate it with the modern concept of energy) threatened to evaporate from a sick person, it was thought that it could be replaced by a drug, in which it occurred in concentrated form. Often the remedy did not even have to be taken; a cure could be effected simply by bringing the material into close contact with the patient's body.

Animism was gradually ousted by 'demonism', which supposed that illness was caused by an evil spirit taking possession of the sick. This gave rise to the notion that the healing and toxic effects of a drug are also due to a demon residing within it. If this demon was powerful enough, it could be used to exorcize the spirit of the disease and, if it were worn or kept in the house, the remedy would actually prevent the spirit of the disease from entering. These notions are still a conscious or unconscious part of folk medicine. Seventeenth-century witchcraft was based on similar ideas, and so was alchemy, the adepts believing that demonic spirits caused chemical reactions.

In the ancient oriental, Egyptian and early Hellenic civilizations, medicine was an esoteric science of the priests, who ascribed the disease and cure to a specific deity. Healing was effected by sleeping in a temple and by other magic rituals, some of which included rational medicinal measures. Temple medicine survived into the Middle Ages as the extravagant cult of the saints: a group of fourteen who

7

were considered to offer help in times of great need were each reputed to have special attributes enabling them to influence the course of a particular disease.

Contemporary with the great Greek philosophers, Hippocrates and his adherents taught that disease is not a fate determined by the gods, but a condition which can be diagnosed and treated with natural medicines by a skilful physician. This view gradually became accepted and led to the discovery and rational exploitation of new drugs.

The medicaments of Antiquity like those mentioned in the writings of Dioscorides (1st century A.D.) came principally from the Mediterranean region, but in the High Middle Ages when Arabic culture reached its zenith, the range of available medicines was extended by drugs from India, Indonesia and South-East Africa. In the 12th and 13th centuries, the translation and interpretation of Arabic writings prompted the founding of medical faculties in the mediaeval universities.

Explorers and missionaries of the modern era have brought us countless new and effective drugs from the New World, Africa and the Far East, and we have still not completed the task of screening and testing all of them.

Chemical preparations also found increasing medical application, although they did not really revolutionize the range of therapeutic agents in common use. Most early physicians were convinced of the infallibility of authority and, until far into the 18th century, official pharmacopoeias were loath to monograph new drugs. They merely reiterated the formulae of antiquated remedies and absurd indications, and coprophagia, theriac with its 80 or more constituents and other panaceas of Antiquity retained pride of place.

This conservatism prevailed until the Age of Enlightenment, a movement which was very much inspired and promulgated on the Continent by the eminent Swiss scholar

Albrecht von Haller. In his foreword to the *Pharmacopoea Helvetica* of 1771, Haller insists that traditional remedies be thoroughly tested on healthy and sick people and only included in the pharmacopoeia if their action does actually tally with the traditional indications.

By this time the sciences of botany and chemistry were developing rapidly. There now followed a golden age of pharmaceutical history in which academic pharmacists emerged as the founders of modern chemistry, and names like Scheele and Sertürner are indelibly printed in the annals of chemistry.

The items and objects on display in the *Schweizerisches Pharmazie-historisches Museum* provide a convenient way of tracing the historical development of drugs. Indeed, it was the many exhibits in this museum which prompted Mrs. Lydia Mez to write this book. As a former curator she is a competent authority on pharmaceutical antiquities. This book, which will be of interest to expert and layman alike, is not intended to be a comprehensive guide to the history of drugs, but merely an attempt to present to the reader some representative aspects of pharmaceutical history. This is achieved by incorporating illustrations of typical objects and items, accompanied by a brief explanation.

Special thanks are due to F. Hoffmann-La Roche & Co. Ltd, 'the world's greatest pharmacy' as they have been called, without whose munificence this publication would not have been possible.

Mesopotamia

Geographically, the land between the Euphrates and Tigris was on many important trade routes and consequently there was lively commercial activity and a far-reaching cultural exchange between its inhabitants and the peoples of neighbouring countries. The borders of Mesopotamia offered very little natural protection. This made it a tempting proposition for military conquest and its history has been one of great turmoil. The first great period was the Sumerian epoch, around 3000–2400 B.C. The thoughts and beliefs of the Sumerians were deeply rooted in an animistic religion. Corporeality was ascribed to natural events, man was a servant of the gods and illness was equated with sin. A sick man was thought to have been smitten by a god and the patient could only be cured (i.e. purified) by expiation. The priest-healers, who were the physicians of the time, were divided into three groups:

1. seers;
2. prophets;
3. physician-priests, who were often surgeons as well.

Later on, other peoples adopted the Sumerian cuneiform script and it became the form of writing for many languages. A number of drug formulae and names have been found on tablets which have survived from the Sumerian period. Professor Kramer of the University of Pennsylvania has identified the drugs cassia, asafoetida, myrtle, thyme, salix, figs and dates in a Sumerian formula. Milk, snake-skin and tortoise-shell were some of the animal products incorporated in other formulae, and minerals used included common salt and saltpetre. Unfortunately, we have no record of the diseases which these medicaments were supposed to combat.

In 2400 B.C., Sargon of Akkad conquered Mesopotamia. The Akkadians soon integrated with the Sumerians to produce a Sumerian-Akkadian culture, a Bronze-Age civilization. In 2025 B.C., the Amorites invaded the country and built their capital in what had hitherto been a minor town, Babylon. The Amorites collected the old myths, epic poems and texts on astrology and medicine and, as the country was now bilingual, the scribes compiled dictionaries. A magnificent document from this period is the legal code of king Hammurabi, which represents the earliest legislation known. This lays down a rigid legal code very much like that found in the Old Testament. Physicians who neglected their patients were severely punished and in serious cases the penalty could be mutilation.

With the advent of the Assyrians, who had been using iron since 1000 B.C., there began a period of great reorganization in Mesopotamia and trade with distant lands flourished.

The cotton-plant was introduced from India. In Mesopotamia weights and measures, which are of great importance in the preparation and dosage of medicinal preparations, were based on a sexuagesimal system which, with certain changes, persisted in the West for centuries until the metric system was introduced. The Assyrians and Babylonians had a vast administrative organization. The thousands of clay tablets which have survived give us an insight into the organization of their state, their trading relations

Roll seal of physician Urlugaledin, Assyrian.
Musée du Louvre, Paris, Antiquit orientales.
Photograph: Service de document tion photographique de la Réunic des Musées nationaux, Château d Versailles.

healing devil Pazuzu.
rian.
sée du Louvre, Paris,
quités orientales.
tograph: Service de documenta-
photographique de la Réunion
Musées nationaux, Château de
sailles.

and wars, and also tell us about their religion and diseases. Deciphering medical texts is fraught with difficulty. Drugs were often given code names referring to a deity or sacred animal, such as 'eye of the sun' or 'skin of the yellow serpent', and magic and astrology sometimes assumed greater importance than drugs. However, many drugs were known and R. Campell Thompson has identified about 250 medicinal plants, 120 minerals and 180 drugs derived from animals. Potent drugs include hellebore, henbane, mandrake, poppy and hemp. Infusions with wine, ointments, enemas, poultices and fumigation were the most common ways of administering drugs.

Tschirch has translated a prescription as follows: 'His right ear is afflicted, it is tympanous and discharging. From the eighth or ninth *ab* (calendar month of August), you should take a fragrant pomegranate which is fixed to a wooden support (meaning a trellis), squeeze out the juice, place inside the ear with sweet oil from the foreign shrub, anoint his head with oil from the foreign shrub; he should eat boiled fish.

'For bronchitis: if the patient is suffering from a wheezing cough, if his windpipe is full of rales, if he coughs, if he suffers bouts of coughing, if he expectorates: pound roses and mustard together, drop it in purified oil on to his tongue, also fill a tube with it and blow it into his nostrils. Then he should drink best beer several times, so he will recover.'

Magic was normally employed in the preparation of drugs. Astrology was intricately bound up with religion, so astrology was also a prominent feature of medical practice.

Medical texts clearly show that Mesopotamian physicians were accurate observers but, because of their particular *Weltanschauung,* they did not develop a scientific approach to thinking.

Frieze from the palace of king Sargon II, in Khorsabad. It dep two priests. The first is carrying gazelle and holding a mandrake flower in his hand; the second i holding poppy heads.
8th century B.C.
Musée du Louvre, Paris, Antiqu orientales.
Photograph: Service de docume tion photographique de la Réun des Musées nationaux, Château Versailles.

Egypt

There are many similarities between the medical writings of Mesopotamia and Egypt. The two cultures developed in much the same way and the art of healing originated from the same magico-religious mode of thought. However, geographical and environmental differences between the two regions produced some important differences in medical practices.

The rational side of medicine developed more in Egypt than in Mesopotamia, where magic remained a prominent feature of the healing art. However, we still come across references to magical charms in Egyptian manuscripts.

ss smelling-bottles from Egypt
the Near East.
lticoloured glass bottles were
erred for cosmetics. They were
blown, but prepared by a sand-
e technique whereby hot glass
ads of many different colours
e wound around a central core
and and clay. Glass production
hed its zenith in Egypt during the
ı dynasty (circa 1400 B.C.). The
sam jar (height 3¼ inches) in the
pe of a column with a palm
ital, dating from the time of the
araoh Amenophis III, was used for
make-up *(kohl)*; the amphora
t below) contained perfume
ight 3¾ inches). The two bottles
the right, an amphora with a zig-
pattern from the Troad (height
inches) and an alabaster (height
inches) from the same region are
n a later period when this tech-
ue of glass-making flourished
ca 500 B.C.).
ksmuseum van Oudheden,
ʏden, Holland.
otograph: F.G. van Veen,
ʏden, Holland.

Horus steles for use against snake-bites and scorpion stings.
In a country like Egypt where medicine and magic were intimately related,
magical epigrams were used to cure and guard against venomous bites. These
incantations were inscribed on images of the young god Horus, son of Isis, the
goddess of magic. The young Horus was stung by a scorpion and then healed by
magical powers, so he was used to symbolize all those who were in danger from,
or had been bitten by serpents or scorpions. When the patient had prayed to
Horus, he would say: 'Remove for me the biting poison which has pervaded the
limbs of NN; may he be saved from this evil by the power of your words'; finally
he identified himself with the god: 'I am Horus, the Saviour'. These steles depict
the young god Horus astride two crocodiles; in his right hand he is holding two
serpents, a scorpion and an antelope and in his left hand two serpents, a scorpion
and a lion. Above him is the grinning, repulsive head of the god Bes. By touching
the face of Horus the patient hoped to be pervaded by the stone's magical power
and that this would combat the burning venom. The steles illustrated here
are of wood (10½ inches high), slate (8 inches, right) and diorite (5 ½ inches);
these come from the Nile Delta.
14th century B.C.
Rijksmuseum van Oudheden, Leyden, Holland.
Photograph: F.G. van Veen, Leyden, Holland.

Apart from the large number of real gods, the Egyptians
saw the world as being inhabited by spirits, demons and
evil powers, and men had to be constantly on their guard.
The healing properties ascribed to water which had been
poured over a statue of Zedher, the Saviour, and then drunk
as a medicinal draught, was an entirely magical concept.

Remains found in burial chambers have given us some
insight into their use of vegetable products. However, the
papyri are the most important source of information about
the history of medicine and drugs. The Edwin Smith Papyrus provides us with abundant evidence of the empirical
thinking, good observation and practical knowledge of
Egyptian physicians, although this document is primarily
a manual of surgical instruction.

The famous Ebers Papyrus, which dates from the 18th
dynasty (first half of the 16th century B. C.),contains a vast
number of drug formulae. There are details of individual
medicinal preparations and also directions for treating
internal diseases, eye diseases and gynaecological and
dermatological disorders. Drugs were undoubtedly the
principal means of treatment, and Egypt was renowned in
the Ancient World for her drugs and poisons. According
to an Ancient Egyptian myth, the fruits of the mandrake

Palettes for eye make-up.
Eye make-up was quite commonly used in Egypt as early as 4000 B.C.
Originally the make-up was supposed to protect the eyes from infection. The
Egyptians ascribed magical powers to objects on which cosmetics were rubbed
down, and they used them as amulets. The slate specimens in the top row are
in the shape of a tortoise (3¼ inches long) and a bulti fish (5½ inches long).
Everyday objects were also used as models, e.g. a ship (3¼ inches long).
The tablet bearing a stylized bird's head (2¼ inches long) in the foreground
was only used as an amulet. The rectangular plate of green mottled stone
(2½ inches long) shows some sign of wear.
All these objects date back to the 4th millenium B.C.
Rijksmuseum van Oudheden, Leyden, Holland.
Photograph: F.G. van Veen, Leyden, Holland.

Pomegranates.

The pomegranate was very popular in Ancient Egypt. Garlands were woven from its fragrant red blossom, a drink was made from the juicy red fruit, and a healing oil was expressed from pomegranate root. The flowers and fruits were put into burial chambers. This illustration shows a natural pomegranate (1½ inches high), a pomegranate flower vase (3¾ inches) of blue-green sand-core glass with a picture of water wells on the upper edge (circa 1400 B.C.) and a white, flat-bottomed alabaster vase (2¾ inches high) with a cover in the shape of a curled pomegranate calyx (Roman period, 1st century B.C.). There is also a specimen of red clayware with white stucco decoration; this came from a burial chamber of the same period. The clay vase with yellow glaze came from the residence of Pharaoh Echnaton in Amarna (2¾ inches high, circa 1350 B.C.).
Rijksmuseum van Oudheden, Leyden, Holland.
Photograph: F. G. van Veen, Leyden, Holland.

had been brought from Nubia and given to a goddess in beer. There is a precise description of the narcotic effect. The goddess becomes intoxicated, her eyes shine and after the sun has risen she is blind.

The Egyptians imported many drugs from countries at the southern end of the Red Sea. These included myrrh and frankincense.

The quantity of a drug is often stated accurately in the formulae and we are also given details of the preparation. Crude drugs were pulverized or boiled and strained. Beer, date wine or milk were used as solvents and a kind of pill was made from honey or bread dough. Egyptian physicians used suppositories to treat the rectum and vagina. Animal products are often included in the formulae, but there are very few mineral drugs. Antimony sulphide, copper acetate and sodium carbonate were used for eye diseases which even then were a scourge of the Egyptians.

Sigerist and other historians believe that physicians prepared their own medicines, but more recent research by F. Jonckheere has produced evidence to show that physicians and the preparers of medicine were separate groups.

In the Ebers Papyrus we find a description of topical administration of an astringent for rectal prolapse: 'For a patient with displacement in the posterior region: boil together myrrh, frankincense and tiger-nut from the garden, *mhht* from the river bank, celery, coriander, oil and salt, place on raw cotton and insert into the rectum.'

The Ebers Papyrus also contains a description of the castor-oil plant, which reads as follows in Dawson's translation: 'List of the properties of the castor-oil plant. It was found in an old book on things useful to mankind. If the husk is crushed in water and placed on an aching head, the head will be cured at once, as though it had never ached.

'Patients suffering from constipation are advised to chew a few seeds with beer and the stool will be expelled from the body.

'The castor-oil plant will promote hair growth in a woman. Crush it, work it into a mass and apply with lard. The woman should anoint her head with it.

'The oil is obtained from the seeds and used in ointment form for wounds with an evil-smelling discharge. If you use the ointment for ten days, the symptoms will disappear as if nothing had happened. Apply the ointment early in the morning to heal the wounds. A genuine remedy, proven a million times over.'

As in Mesopotamia, the priests were also the physicians. They were a powerful caste in the land of the

Containers for ophthalmological preparations.
In Egypt there were specialists as well as general practitioners and veterinary surgeons. The most well-known specialist was the ophthalmologist, who had a great deal to do in the hot Egyptian climate. At home, people treated their eyes with preparations which were kept in small medicine chests, and it is difficult to distinguish here between cosmetic and medicinal use. The container on the left is made of ebony and consists of five tubes for storing the preparations (height 3¼ inches). The name of the owner appears on the flat part between two tubes: 'the scribe Tetiti'. According to the inscription, the left-hand tube contained a preparation to prevent squint, and the right-hand tube contained one to stop tears; the other tubes contained preparations to 'open the vision' and a 'cosmetic for general everyday use'. The right-hand container is made of brown-black stone with a white alabaster cover (height 2½ inches). The preparations were applied with wooden or bronze spatulas.
18th dynasty, circa 1400 B.C.
Rijksmuseum van Oudheden, Leyden, Holland.
Photograph: F.G. van Veen, Leyden, Holland.

Containers for ointments and oils.
From left to right, back row: vase, alabaster, for eye make-up *(kohl)*.
Middle Kingdom, circa 1800 B.C.
Height 3 inches.
Alabaster tube in the shape of a palm column, for cosmetics.
18th dynasty, circa 1350 B.C. Length 3¾ inches.
Spherical alabaster pot bearing the names Pharaoh Amenophis and Queen Teje,
the parents of Echnaton.
Circa 1375 B.C. Height 1¾ inches.
Cylindrical alabaster ointment pot bearing the name Queen Hatshepsut.
Circa 1480 B.C.
Alabaster for ointments and perfume, from the Greek period.
Height 3¼ inches.
Left foreground, a tube for *kohl,* blue faience; there is a thread of yellow glass
wound around the base. Height 3½ inches.
Centre: ebony powder box with an ivory lid. Height 1½ inches.
Right: perfume bottle of blue-green faience. Height 1¼ inches.
Rijksmuseum van Oudheden, Leyden, Holland.
Photograph: F. G. van Veen, Leyden, Holland.

Formulae on a medico-magical papyrus.

The Egyptians believed that disease was the work of an evil spirit. A cure depended on the power which could be wielded over this spirit, and so magic spells were used to heal the sick. The physician was a magician and he uttered incantations over various concoctions and mixtures. These mixtures sometimes had an intrinsic curative action, but more commonly they were a hotchpotch of bizarre substances. When the preparation had been thus endowed with magical properties, it was applied to the affected part of the body or taken internally. Many incantations and formulae have survived the centuries on papyrus scrolls. The illustration shows a fragment from a medico-magical papyrus. The text is hieratic and it dates from the time of Rameses II (circa 1250 B.C.). Here the patient, who has received a head wound, is identified with Horus 'the avenger of his father' (Osiris). 'He is Horus, o gods, the Lord of Life, who rightfully approaches the house of his father! That no god or goddess, neither male nor female spirit, neither dead man nor dead woman, nor any evil being, male or female, shall be able to take possession of the limbs of the son of any woman, whomsoever he may be, to perpetrate anything evil or bad.'

Then, written in red ink, directions for using this incantation: 'To be uttered over the talons of a falcon, over the shell of a tortoise. Boil it and put it in oil. Anoint a wounded man (with it) on the site of his wounds. No evil or bad will befall him. A reliable remedy, proven a million times over.'

Rijksmuseum van Oudheden, Leyden, Holland.

Photograph: F. G. van Veen, Leyden, Holland.

pharaohs and were very secretive about their medical knowledge. Treatment was combined with sacred rites which were often incomprehensible to the patient. The ritual of hygiene dominated the entire public medical welfare service and the private lives of the Egyptians.

All the old deities possessed the power of healing, notably Thoth, who was also Physician to the Gods. Imhotep, who was later deified, probably lived during the 3rd dynasty. He is reputed to be the architect of the step pyramid of Saqqarah and must have been a gifted physician. Imhotep is probably the first physician we know by name and his reputation was such that, like Aesculapius, he was revered as a god.

The influence of Egyptian medicine must have been profound and far-reaching. The private physicians of the Persian king Darius were Egyptians, and Egyptians were then reputed to be the best physicians in the world. There was probably a lively exchange of knowledge and ideas between Egyptian and Greek physicians, but it is difficult to tell how far back the influence of the Egyptians extended. Later on, a great deal of the knowledge was preserved in Coptic writings. According to Bouriant, one Coptic manuscript from the 9th or 10th century A.D. contains 237 formulae which are very closely allied to their Ancient Egyptian counterparts.

lk container in the shape of a
›ther and child.

ıe or two vessels which have sur-
·ed from the 18th dynasty (circa
ɔ B.C.) were designed to hold the
lk of a mother who had given
·th to a healthy male child. This
lk was specifically recommended
Egyptian physicians as a remedy
· sick children. The vessels are
hioned in the shape of the arche-
ɔal mother, the goddess Isis, whose
lk cured the sick child Horus.
ıeir shape and the magical incanta-
ns uttered over them led people
believe that it was possible for the
ntents to be transformed into an
ective drug. The example
ıstrated is of red terracotta and
·mes from Thebes.
·ight 5 inches.
jksmuseum van Oudheden,
yden, Holland.
otograph: F.G. van Veen,
yden, Holland.

Greece and Rome

We have very little evidence about the use of medicines during the heroic period. Gods and men inflicted appalling wounds on Homer's heroes, but there is little or no mention of their being treated medicinally. Apollo sent the plague into the Achaean camp with his deadly arrows. The god had to be appeased with a sacrifice and the epidemic then died down. This concept of spiritual purification was akin to the magico-religious ideas of the highly sophisticated Mesopotamian and Egyptian civilizations. Magic potions and poisons are frequently mentioned in Greek myths, but the word *pharmakon* meant not only a fatal poison but

also a substance which brought some relief from pain or arrested bleeding.

Gods endowed with the power of healing included Apollo and Asklepios. In the course of time, Asklepios became the tutelary god of physicians and persons skilled in the art of healing, and temples dedicated to him were erected in many parts of Greece. Epidaurus, Cos and Pergamos were centres of the cult of Asklepios. His pupils and followers were known as the Asklepiadae, the most famous of these being Hippocrates.

Indirectly, the Greek philosophers had a decisive influence on medical trends. They were not content simply to observe nature. They sought an explanation and the root cause of things. This completely new mode of thought gradually released medicine from the shackles of magic.

Hippocrates is reputed to have been born on the island of Cos in about 460 B.C. Little is known of his life or work, and the only evidence we have is in the dialogues of Plato. Over the centuries a number of legends have grown up about Hippocrates himself and his work, and these have made Hippocrates the most influential of Greek physicians. Later on, the Alexandrian School assembled all the known medical literature and produced the *Corpus Hippocraticum*, which contains a vast collection of accurately observed clinical symptoms, dietetic treatments supported by medicinal adjuncts, and theories as to the nature of mankind. However, there was still no actual textbook of medicaments. The Hippocratic oath was probably written later.

The School of Alexandria concentrated mainly on the acquisition of theoretical knowledge, but there were also the empiricists who rejected techniques of speculation and based their healing methods on experience.

The greatest physicians in Rome were nearly all Greek. Dioscorides was a contemporary of the Emperors Claudius and Nero (1st century A.D.), and in his *Materia medica* he

red relief.
gment from a sacred relief
icated to Asklepios.
telic marble.
ic, circa 330 B.C.
ght 15 inches.
ikenmuseum, Basle,
. B.S. 1906/58.
otograph: P. Heman, Basle.

Roman cosmetics-medicine ches
Bronze. Found in Cologne, Mela
gürtel. First half of the 3rd centu
1 ½ inches high, 5 inches long,
3 inches deep.
Römisch-Germanisches Museum
Cologne.

...ium.
...ne, Attic tetradrachm.
...: silphium plant with leaves and
...som.
...: Jupiter Ammon.
...a 480 B.C. Diameter 1 inch.
...ection of Dr. A.Lutz, Basle.
...tograph: P.Heman, Basle.

describes nearly 500 plants and remedies prepared from animals and metals. He also gives precise instructions for preparing drugs. Dioscorides accompanied the Roman armies through Spain, North Africa and Syria, and on these journeys he probably learnt of many new drugs. He was a genuine natural scientist, a keen observer who examined traditional beliefs for scientific validity. The famous *Codex Constantinopolitanus*, written in about A.D. 510 in Constantinople and now in Vienna, contains lifelike illustrations of the most important medicinal plants known at the time of Dioscorides. His work is the most important source of pharmacognostical knowledge from Antiquity.

Pliny the Elder, who was killed in A.D. 79 when Vesuvius erupted, also made an interesting contribution to the history of drugs in that he compiled a kind of encyclopaedia of contemporary knowledge, which contains a great deal of information about medicinal plants and remedies.

The influence of Galen (A.D. 130–201) extended far beyond his own era. He was born in Pergamos and started his career as physician to the gladiators in his home town. Later he travelled through Asia Minor and went to Alexandria, which was then the centre of medicine. In about A.D. 164 he moved to Rome, but was forced to leave four years later because of disputes with resident physicians. He again travelled for a year before Marcus Aurelius appointed him private physician to the Imperial Family. Galen died in Sicily between A.D. 200 and 201.

Galen recognized the value of medicinal plants and he introduced many hitherto unknown drugs. He believed that crude drugs should be considered in terms of their place of origin, and the physician should decide for himself what qualities they possess. He divided drugs into three groups:

1. those with the basic effects of warmth, coldness, moistness or dryness;

Arkesilas bowl.

In ancient times the silphium plant was in great demand and was exported from Cyrene in North Africa. It was probably completely destroyed by uncontrolled cutting and we can no longer say for certain what the plant silphium was. Some authorities believe it was thapsia, an umbelliferous plant. Its juice was used as a condiment and medicine.

Work of a painter of Arkesilas, circa 565–560 B.C.

Bibliothèque nationale, Cabinet des médailles, Paris.

Photograph: Hirmer Fotoarchiv, Munich.

2. those in which the principal effect and subsidiary effect are combined in various ways;
3. those with a specific action attributable to the intrinsic qualities of the substance.

Galen defined a drug as being anything which acts on the body to bring about a change, as opposed to foods which increase the substance of the body.

Galen believed that disease was a manifestation of change in the function of individual components of the body and that disease was due to a change in the humours. According to Galen, the fluid constituents, i.e. the humours, were: blood, phlegm, yellow bile and black bile, and these corresponded to the four elements as follows: fire: yellow bile, liver. This is hot and dry and predominates in cholerics. Earth: black bile, spleen, the attribute of melancholics. Water: phlegm, brain, moist and cold, characteristic of phlegmatics. Air: blood and heart, the nature of sanguine people. Drugs were prescribed according to whether the patient required a hot or cold remedy. Many medicinal plants are mentioned in Galen's treatise *On diets to dilute the humours*. Another of his texts is devoted to the wonder drug, theriac.

Galen had a tremendous influence on the medicine of later centuries. Until modern times he was considered to be the true apostle of medicine. Paracelsus was the first to dare to criticize his writings.

Galen was the most important figure amongst the physicians of Antiquity, but the work of Celsus was also very influential, and North Africa, a very important cultural centre in the 4th century A.D., produced Vindicianus, friend of Saint Augustine, and his pupil Priscianus and also Cassius Felix from Carthage. In A.D. 410, the Gaul Marcellus of Bordeaux wrote his book *De medicamentis*, which includes not only classical drugs, but also writings about the indigenous Celtic medicine.

...dea sarcophagus (part of the lid).
...sorceress Medea is using a
...ping draught to drug the serpent
...rding the golden fleece. On the
...Jason is about to steal the fleece.
...illustration shows the right
...t side of the sarcophagus lid.
...ght of lid: 12 inches.
...nan imperial period, circa
...190.
...ikenmuseum, Basle, No. B.S. 203.
...tograph: P. Heman, Basle.

Theriac

In collaboration with his private physician, Mithridates VI Eupator, king of Pontus (132–63 B.C.), is reputed to have compounded 54 substances into a universal antidote against poisoning. This was called the mithridate. The formula is said to have been brought to Rome by Pompey after his defeat of the king. Andromachus, one of Nero's private physicians, improved the formula and Galen passed it on under the name Theriac of Andromachus. By this time it contained 64 ingredients, one of the most important constituents being pills made from the flesh of vipers. Galen recommended theriac as an antidote for snake-bites. In the

...riac jar with handles of inter-
...ed serpents.
...chrome painting.
...ice, 18th century.
...ght 15 inches.
...weizerisches Pharmazie-
...orisches Museum, Basle.
...tograph: P. Heman, Basle.

Formulae written on parchment,
including a formula for theriac.
From a Roman Jesuit pharmacy,
1621.
22 × 35 ½ inches.
Schweizerisches Pharmazie-
historisches Museum, Basle.
Photograph: P. Heman, Basle.

Drachm.
Obv.: portrait of king Mithridates
Eupator, king of Pontus.
Diameter ¾ inch.
Collection of Dr. A. Lutz, Basle.
Photograph: P. Heman, Basle.

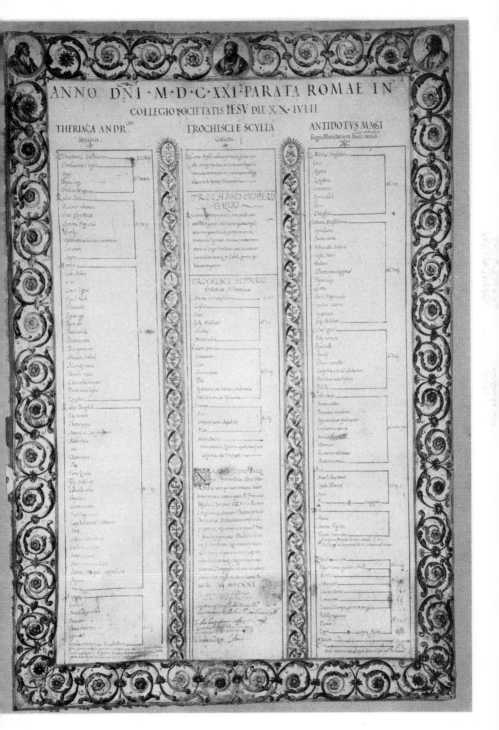

ANNO · DÑI · M·D·C·XXI · PARATA ROMAE IN
COLLEGIO SOCIETATIS IESV DIE XX· IVLII

course of time, like the philosopher's stone of the alchemists, theriac became the panacea for curing all diseases
and it was still in medicinal use until late into the 18th century. To prevent fraudulent practices, in many cities including Venice, Montpellier and Toulouse, theriac was
prepared in public under official supervision. To this day
there are magnificent flat-bottomed jars in old pharmacies
and museums as evidence of the importance accorded to
this wonder drug.

Mandragora

The mandrake, *Mandragora officinalis* L. (Solanaceae), from the Mediterranean region was highly prized by the Babylonians and Egyptians for its narcotic action. The plant *dudaim* mentioned in the Old Testament (Genesis 30, 14) may also have been mandragora. In his medical treatises Aulus Cornelius Celsus (1st century A.D.) alludes to the fruits of the mandragora as a potent hypnotic and recommends boiling the root for treatment of blennorrhoea of the eyes and toothache. The shape of the mandrake rhizome has aroused the imagination of men through the ages because the tap-root is often anthropomorphous, with arms and legs. In a manuscript from Roman times we find instructions about digging up the root: 'A man should not do it, because it would endanger his life. Therefore the top part of the plant is tied to a black dog, and the animal has to be driven until the mandragora is lifted out of the earth. At this moment the plant will utter a terrible shriek and the dog will fall dead on the spot. To survive, the root gatherer must plug his ears with wax beforehand.'

The reputation of this drug, which is the subject of so many legends, persists to this day. It has often been stated to have an aphrodisiac effect. At the end of the Middle Ages and during the Renaissance there was a genuine mandrake cult. This and other familiar magic plants were important ingredients in the preparation of the notorious witches' unguent. Enormous prices were asked for this drug and charlatans peddled substitutes including long-rooted garlic *(Allium victoriale* L.) and bryony *(Bryonia alba* L.). Mandrake was often worn as an amulet. It was supposed to protect the wearer from sickness, and to bring him wealth and happiness. Incantations were often uttered over it and, to increase the price still further, many dealers claimed that the plants would only grow under gallows, at the feet of a hanged man.

Dog helping to pull up mandragora root.
Voss. lat. 949, f 46 v.
Bibliothek der Rijksuniversiteit te Leyden, Holland.

...re of a monkey fashioned out of
...dragora (bryony) root.
...ght 7½ inches.
...weizerisches Pharmazie-
...orisches Museum, Basle.
...tograph: P. Heman, Basle.

The Arabs

During the 7th century, the Arabs conquered the Near East, Persia, part of the Middle East and the coast of North Africa, at the beginning of the 8th century they occupied Spain and in 827 they captured Sicily. In India, Islam penetrated as far as the Malay Archipelago. So the Mohammedan religion extended from Spain to South-East Asia.

The Arab conquerers were very ready to assimilate the knowledge and culture of nations they had vanquished.

In the province of Syria, which was initially Roman and later Byzantine, there were schools at which one of the subjects taught was medicine. In A.D. 431, the Council of Ephesus condemned followers of the patriarch Nestorius as heretics and many Syrian Nestorian Christians emigrated to Nisibis and Gondêschâpûr in Persia. Whilst in Syria, they had translated Greek manuscripts into their own tongue, and they continued this tradition in Persia. In Gondêschâpûr they founded hospitals which taught practical medicine. Both Christian and Jewish authors translated the works of ancient civilizations into Arabic and in this way the knowledge of Antiquity filtered through Syria to Persia and finally to the Arabs.

In 763, the Abbasids made Baghdad their capital and this became a flourishing cultural centre under Haroun al Rashid (786–809), a contemporary of Charlemagne. The caliphs summoned physicians from Gondêschâpûr, built hospitals and founded libraries. Arabic medicine was very specialized and the work load had to be shared between physicians and the preparers of medicines. One of the main reasons for this was the advent of polypharmacy, the Arabic formulae sometimes containing over 100 individual drugs. The pharmacy is an Arab institution which first came into existence in Baghdad.

From the 8th century on, the Arabs dominated trade in the Indian Ocean and the caravan routes from India and Africa. A number of new drugs were imported and added to the armamentarium of medicaments. These included rhubarb, camphor, senna, sandalwood, nutmeg, tamarind, clove and ambergris.

One of the greatest of the Arab physicians, Rhazes (865–925), was a Persian born in Rayy near Teheran. His teaching was based on traditional knowledge and on his own clinical observations. He worked in one of the largest hospitals in Baghdad and he is said to have had many students. His principal work, a compilation of his own experience, *Al-hâwi*, 'the storehouse', was published posthumously. In the 12th century a Latin translation of this

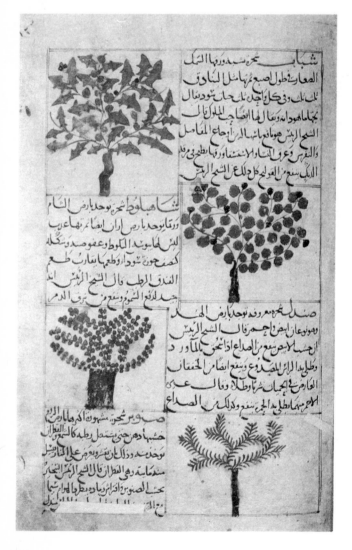

Miracle of creation of Quaswini. Illustration of plants.
Arabic. Cod. arab. 464, fol. 120. Bayerische Staatsbibliothek, Mun Photograph: Handschriftenabtei lung, Bayerische Staatsbibliothek Munich.

work appeared under the title *Liber Continens,* and this was to play an important part in medicine of the Western world. Rhazes is noted for the independence of his thought. On the use of drugs he wrote: 'If you can help with foods, i.e. by dietary means, then do not prescribe medicaments, and if simples are effective, then do not prescribe compounded remedies.'

Ali ibn Sina (Latin name Avicenna) was also a Persian (980–1037) and author of books on philosophy, natural history and medicine. His *Canon medicinae,* a comprehensive textbook divided into five books, is a synopsis of Greek

and Roman medicine. The influence of Galen is unmistakable, but he also incorporates many of his own observations. In the centuries which followed, the *Canon* of Avicenna became one of the authoritative textbooks and it was held in the same esteem as the works of Hippocrates and Galen.

New centres of learning grew up in North Africa (Kairouan) and in Moorish Spain (Córdoba). Hispano-Moorish thought tended to be more independent than that in the Eastern regions. In the 10th century, Córdoba was an influential cultural centre and the Moorish rulers founded libraries and schools of learning. The private library of caliph Al-Mustansir (after 950) is reputed to have contained more than 400,000 volumes.

The outstanding Moorish scholar of the 10th century, Al-Zahrāwī (known as Albucasis), was born in Córdoba in about 940 and died in about the year 1000. He wrote a comprehensive volume entitled *Al-Tasrīf* containing a great deal of pharmaceutical material, although for a long time only the treatise on surgery was known in the West. Gerhard of Cremona translated this section of the book into Latin. He worked in Toledo, where there was a famous school of translators which was instrumental in passing on Arab learning to the West.

More recent research work has shown that Albucasis' work embraced all that was then known about medicine. In fact, his *Al-Tasrif* is a medical encyclopaedia with important sections on the preparation and effects of medicaments.

One of the most independent minds in Arab medicine was Ibn Rusd, who was born in 1126 in Córdoba and known as Averroës. The Jewish doctor Mose ben Maimon, known as Maimonides (1135–1204), also came from Córdoba. He was forced to leave Spain of the Almohads because of religious intolerance. He went to Cairo and

Canon of Avicenna. Codex 2197. Illustration showing a pharmacy. Insets: sunbathing, three bathing scenes; cupping; bleeding; proba illustrates thoracic puncture. Hebr Biblioteca universitaria di Bologna

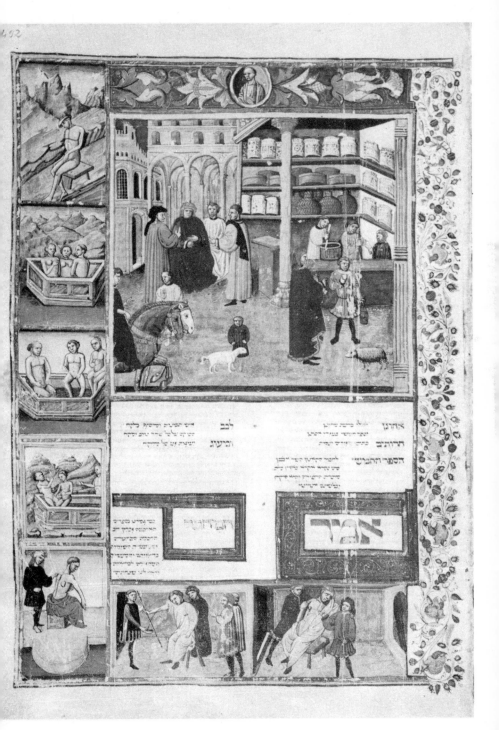

there became private physician to the family of Sultan Saladin.

Of the Moorish scholars, Ibn Baithar from Malaga was the greatest authority on medicinal plants. He made extensive study tours through North Africa, Egypt and Asia Minor and for a time was private physician in Cairo at the court of the caliph. His textbook on drugs includes all the *materia medica* known at that time and about 200 new drugs are mentioned. He based his work on Dioscorides and Galen, but also incorporated many of his own observations. Ibn Baithar died in 1248.

Arab medicine only flourished for a few centuries. The Arabs achieved greatness by establishing comprehensive libraries and founding hospitals and schools of learning. However, because of an acceptance of authoritarian dogma, scientific thought tended to become inflexible and this proved a great obstacle to the development of rational empiricism. Nevertheless, the authoritative works of the great Arab physicians, which also incorporated a good deal of ancient philosophy, acted as a stimulant to Western medicine. Knowledge added later directly from Greek sources by Humanism and the Renaissance did not contribute greatly to pharmacy.

Arab medicine was largely responsible for the development of pharmaceutics. They introduced and refined techniques such as evaporation, filtration and distillation. The alembic used for distillation goes back to the Arabs. Rhazes is reputed to have used mercury compounds therapeutically and Arab pharmacists introduced a series of new dosage forms, including concentrated vegetable sap in pill form (called roob), julep, a mild cooling syrup, candied fruits, juices sweetened with sugar, electuaries and gilded or silvered pills.

The word *al-cohol* means 'all things very fine', and originally it referred to finely ground galena and antimony

sulphide which was used as eye make-up. The Arabs did
not succeed in distilling alcohol, but they were masters at
preparing fragrant essences, particularly rose-water.

Alchemy

To ancient civilizations, gold represented the sun on earth and the sun was the supreme deity. To the alchemists gold had a dual nature, secular and sacred. Their ideas were based on the teaching of Aristotle that all substances are only different forms of the same fundamental substance. Alchemistic writers in Alexandria tried to combine Egyptian ideas, astronomy, astrology and Greek natural philosophy with Christian metaphysics, in order to discover the origin and meaning of all things. The production of gold from base materials was regarded as a process of spiritual purification.

The alchemists used a highly symbolic language and the symbols often had several meanings. Gold represented not only the sun but also the male principle. Silver was both the moon and the female. Sulphur corresponded to fire and the sun, and mercury to the moon. The 'grey wolf' meant antimony, the 'white eagle' sal ammoniac, the 'black crow' lead and the 'green lion' glass.

The fundamental substance, *materia prima,* corresponded to chaos and was composed of the four elements water, fire, earth and air. However, in these there was a fifth substance which made it possible for the precious, i.e. gold, to be extracted from the base. This *Quinta essentia* was the philosopher's stone.

The aim of alchemy was to discover gold by the magistery, the 'master principle of nature'. This process was divided into seven stages, namely calcination, putrefaction, sublimation, solution, distillation, coagulation and tincture. Each of these processes was controlled by a planet or the appropriate metal. For example, distillation came under the sign of Venus and her metal was copper.

The transmutation of base materials into precious substances was an idea adopted by Christian mystics and the death and resurrection of Christ was closely linked with the alchemistic concept of purification.

Peacock's tail and children of V.
The seven stages of the 'master
principle of nature', i.e. transmu
tion and purification, correspon
to the seven planets. A metal wa
ascribed to each planet. The sym
in this picture are associated wi
Venus. The Venus chariot appea
the top of the picture, around th
retort there are groups of lovers
children of Venus. The peacock
the astrological sign of Venus a
the peacock plume symbolizes a
stage of transmutation through
the shades of yellow-red to purp
From the *Splendor solis*, an illustr
manuscript of alchemy from the
mid-16th century.
Germanisches Nationalmuseum
Nuremberg.

Regeneration of the old king in h
son, an alchemistic symbol of
renewal.
According to the alchemistic myt
the regal metal gold had to be
destroyed for there to be regenerat
in a new form. The dove is a symb
of the Holy Spirit, the Holy Ghos
From the *Splendor solis*, an illustra
manuscript of alchemy from the
mid-16th century.
Germanisches Nationalmuseum,
Nuremberg.

Many distinguished scholars of the Middle Ages and Renaissance were alchemists, the most renowned of these being Albertus Magnus, Raimondo Lull, Arnald of Villanova, Paracelsus and Glauber. They believed in transmutation of the *materia prima* by alchemy. Their motive was far from being mere greed. The work of a genuine alchemist was an entirely ethical investigation, but braggarts and charlatans, the 'goldmakers' who turned up at some time in every country, brought alchemy into disrepute. Cajetanus, who was executed in Kustrin in 1709, was an example of this. The most celebrated of these dubious adepts was Giuseppe Balsamo, born in Palermo in 1743 and known by the pretentious name of Count Cagliostro.

Alchemy and alchemistic speculation became of great practical importance in the preparation of medicines and later in chemistry. Distillation was one of the main processes used in the adepts' laboratories. From old equipment and illustrations in books on alchemy we know that over the centuries the ovens, flasks, retorts, crucibles, etc. were constantly being improved and the modern apparatus in our chemical laboratories developed from the alchemist's kitchen.

Chinese as alchemist.

el from the *Grande Singerie* in Château de Chantilly. The paint-is in the chinoiserie style. The emist is seen at work in his oratory. In the foreground left right he has two apes as his stants and there is a small distilla-unit. Other laboratory apparatus n the shelves. Top left there is a fed crocodile and on the right ake. Bellows, a sieve and a funnel hanging from the ceiling. nting by Christophe Huet, who 1 in 1759.
iteau de Chantilly.
otograph: Photographie audon, Paris VIᵉ.

The Middle Ages

Even after the fall of the Roman Empire in the West, the
threads of ancient tradition were never completely severed,
and this also applied to medicine. An important personality,
who played a vital role in the further development of medicine, came to prominence in the Ostrogothic Empire. He
was Aurelius Cassiodorus (490–580), chancellor of Theo-
doric the Great. He attempted to found a university in
Rome, but his plans never came to fruition. After resigning
his posts, Cassiodorus withdrew completely from public
life. In 540 he founded an academy in Calabria, on the
Gulf of Squillace, modelling it upon the schools of Syria

and Alexandria. The study of medicine was specifically mentioned in the statutes of organization and teaching was based on the works of Galen and Dioscorides.

In Visigothic Spain, the learned bishop of Seville, Isidore (560–636) compiled an encyclopaedia of 20 volumes, the *Etymologies*. Two of the books are devoted to medicine.

After the migration of the peoples, most of the educated in the West were clergy. Their approach to healing was based primarily on the concept of Christian charity, and scientific observation took second place. The monks were familiar with a good deal of ancient learning, but their medicine and pharmacy were based largely on empiricism.

Many monasteries had buildings for housing the sick, and a medicinal herb garden. The Benedictine monks were mainly responsible for bringing Roman horticultural techniques from Italy to the rest of Europe. Walafrid Strabo (809–849), at Reichenau, wrote didactic poems in hexameters containing information about the rearing, cultivation and use of medicinal herbs known at that time.

Gerbert of Aurillac, later Pope Sylvester II, provided a great stimulus to scientific thought amongst the clergy. In about 967 he had visited Spain and the progress made by the Arabs in all fields of learning made a deep impression on him. As well as many other new ideas, Gerbert is reputed to have introduced Arabic numerals into Western countries.

One of the treatises of the abbess Hildegard of Bingen (1098–1179) was a textbook of *materia medica* which, although influenced by ancient writings, also contains a great deal of information about folk medicine. Among the indigenous medicinal herbs she mentions are marsh-mallow, valerian, absinth, levisticum, thyme, dandelion, St. John's wort, coltsfoot, lavender and poppy.

Medical knowledge was preserved in the monasteries by the monks' work of copying and compiling material. The drugs used were very simple and mostly of vegetable origin. The entire plant or parts of it, such as roots, leaves or seeds, were used in the preparation. Formulae often do not give precise details as to quantity or weight, and instructions such as 'a handful, a bundle, a cup' had to suffice. Many drugs were prepared by decoction or maceration, and electuaries and wafers were favourite dosage forms.

Jörimann classifies formularies of the early Middle Ages into antidotaria and formularia. In antidotaria, after the name there is a list of indications which reveals the antitoxic character of the antidote. Preparation was complicated and costly. In contrast to these the actual formularies

nble bush.
med. graec. 1, fol. 83.
a A.D. 510.
erreichische Nationalbibliothek,
na.
ograph: Bildarchiv der Öster-
hischen Nationalbibliothek,
na.

included many indigenous drugs which were easy to procure. Religious and magical concepts were prominent features of the formularia. People had to cross themselves or recite a magic spell when picking a plant and specific saints were often invoked as well.

Precious drugs included pulverized pearl, and gold and silver figured prominently in the preparation of antidotes. The use of metals like gold was a link with alchemy, and drinkable gold was a principle related to the 'Great Elixir', the magistery.

The tradition of monastery schools was carried on by scholars from the universities. However, these scholars also assimilated a good deal of Arab learning. They were learned and thorough but, as regards medicine, the ground they prepared was rather unproductive since their scholasticism was inclined to relapse into sophistry and, all too often, independent thought became bedevilled by philosophical or philological controversy.

Albertus Magnus, Count von Bollstädt (1193–1280), was an outstanding character of independent mind amongst the scholars of Germany and he embodied the whole of mediaeval science. Albertus was a Dominican, he studied in Padua and taught in Cologne, Würzburg and Strasbourg.

Using peony to treat sciatica.
CPV 93, fol. 72.
13th century.
Österreichische Nationalbiblioth
Vienna.
Photograph: Bildarchiv der Öster
reichischen Nationalbibliothek,
Vienna.

From the Codex Guta Sintram.
Advice for the month of June: dr
fresh water; abstain from beer, m
and mead. To prevent inflammati
of the eyes, drink a decoction of
sage. Use vine and elder blossom.
Circa 1154.
Grand Séminaire, Strasbourg.
Photograph: Archives et Bibliothèque de la ville de Strasbourg.

Wolfhelm Cunradus   Chelmus Cppo abb Rantboldus   Vtho Wernher Cunrat Reiort

66

Agreis os   pentozoton
Sicut uocit   aglofotis
Alii   peonia
Inuenta peonia nom auctores retinent.

Dosat crete -gscue montu; que omer. auctor libnc sue mseruit]nacun
tur plunmu apastorib; b hba in extrema hiatula bt maligninati ma
gnitudine que noctu sic uicet tã lucñam; qd e granu acca sis plunm'
noctu a pastorib; inuentu'; collegetur:

Comerus. auctor   crete sicilia

Pastores; pastores

67

He viewed natural science as *Scientia experimentalis* and, as one of the great researchers of the Middle Ages, his work was directly relevant to medicine. In his books on minerals he alludes to the curative action of various stones and he recommends pulverized chrysolite for treating scabies, and haematite for disorders of the bladder. His book *De vegetabilis* is the work of an extremely observant botanist. He gives accurate descriptions of medicinal herbs and details of their action. However, his thinking tended to be very metaphysical in that he interpreted natural events in terms of supernatural powers.

The Catalan Arnald of Villanova (1235–1311) was a prominent figure in medicine of the High Middle Ages. His writings show that he was an experienced doctor who strove to put scholastic medicine on a rational footing. He opposed those who blindly accepted authoritarian dogma, and relied first and foremost on his practical experience. However, Arnald was greatly influenced by mysticism and astrology and he took the view that medicinal substances are endowed with curative powers by favourable astrological conjunctions.

Arnald wrote many books, the *Breviarium practicae* and *Parables of the art of healing* being worthy of special mention. Villanova also recognized the importance of alchemy in the preparation of pharmaceuticals, but he was not able to make practical use of his knowledge.

The Spanish mystic and alchemist Raimondo Lull (1235–1316) studied in Paris and Montpellier and later he worked as a missionary in the Orient. On returning to Europe he became deeply involved in alchemy. He succeeded in distilling alcohol, which he named in alchemistic fashion *Anima coelica, Mercurius vegetabilis* or *Quinta essentia*. He distilled ammonium carbonate from fermenting urine. Lull was a pioneer in the preparation of tinctures and quintessences in the modern sense.

ian albarello.
a 1300.
smuseum, Amsterdam.
tograph: Reproduktieverkoop,
smuseum, Amsterdam.

Amulets, talismans and magic plants

From time immemorial amulets, talismans and magic plants
have been used as magico-religious objects for warding off
evil, and they feature prominently in the history of primitive and advanced civilizations. Since talismans and amulets were, *per se*, attributed with magical powers, it was
natural that they should be used as protection against disease, or for healing the sick. The talisman was fastened to
the wearer with the idea that it would bring luck and its
effectiveness was thought to depend largely on astrological
factors. 'Birthstones' are an example of talismans still in
use today.

Amulets were supposed to ward off sickness and calamity. It was popularly believed that many illnesses were caused by evil spirits or by malevolent fellow beings, and that their evil influence could be exorcized by secret use of certain signs, by magic herbs or by certain minerals. The doctrine of 'signatures' may also have governed the choice of certain remedies, for example gold was a proven treatment for jaundice, the colour of the metal being the vital factor here, and speckled plants or stones were used to dispel physical blemishes. There were countless different kinds of amulet and it is only possible to mention one or two of the more familiar here. Amulets for protection against the 'evil eye, enchanting and bewitching' (apotropaion) were often in glaring colours and decorated with eyes or three running legs. Pointed objects, such as small horns and branches of coral were also reputed to be effective against bewitching. A familiar form was the *Fical*, with the thumb between second and third finger; this also had an obscene meaning. Malachite, agate, ibex horn and star coral were said to ease delivery, and agate was reputed to give protection against gout. There were many magical agents for use against infantile convulsions, convulsive twitching in young children. The *Fraiskette*, a chain hung

Horseshoe nails.
Horseshoe nails were important objects in folk medicine. White ▼ in which iron nails had been laid for a time was given as a drink t treat anaemia. On the basis of th doctrine of 'signatures', the rust-colour of the liquid was evidence its blood-forming action. Horses nails under the pillow were supp to mitigate pain, and it was thou that a disease could be exorcize knocking a horseshoe nail into a tree-trunk.
Schweizerisches Pharmazie-historisches Museum, Basle.
Photograph: P. Heman, Basle.

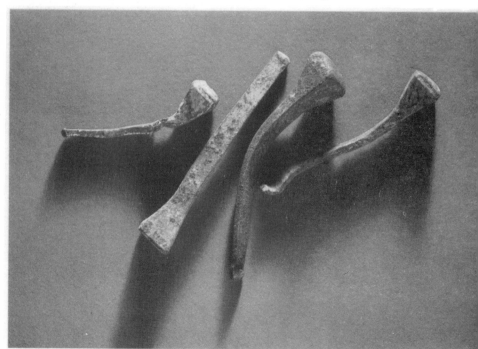

round the child's neck, was supposed to be particularly effective against this ailment, an iron nail under the pillow might relieve or even prevent convulsions and sometimes the act of touching a magic object was said to be enough to effect a cure.

Certain drugs or medicinal plants were part of the charm to drive away the spirits of disease. Plants used included mandragora, yellow-berried mistletoe, rue and garlic. Mandragora and henbane were used for 'witches' ointments'. Many of these magic plants were later used medicinally.

...let.
...ded copper pendant suspended ...n a perforated rosette. In the ...rt-shaped mounting there is a ...wned saint with a palm branch, ...nted in *verre églomisé*.
...n century.
...gth 4½ inches.
...weizerisches Pharmazie- ...orisches Museum, Basle.
...tograph: P. Heman, Basle.

73

Sacred herbal wreaths protected people and animals from sickness. Objects dedicated to certain saints, for instance crosses and medallions, are still used today to ward off certain diseases. Small pictures of the madonna, *Schluckhelgen*, were eaten by patients in the same way as wafers. For centuries St. Antony the Hermit was looked on as the protector against St. Anthony's fire (ergotism). His sign, a Greek T, was worn around the neck as an amulet. Objects dedicated to Saint Sebastian and Saint Rochus were regarded as being particularly effective against plague. Pendants with mysterious inscriptions are some of

Star coral.
Verschreiherz or 'scabies stone' for use against skin eruptions in children. Heart-shaped star coral, polished on one side, of grey madpore calcium. The two loops and pendant ring are fashioned like coiled rope.
Height 2 inches.
Schweizerisches Pharmazie-historisches Museum, Basle.
Photograph: P. Heman, Basle.

plague sachets.
y contain medicinal herbs and
ue charms printed on paper.
ton of Lucerne, 17th century.
× 3 inches and 2 ¼ × 2 ¼ inches.
weizerisches Pharmazie-
orisches Museum, Basle.
tograph: P. Heman, Basle.

the oldest healing amulets known, and even letters of safe conduct containing the blessing of Benedict or Zachariah (forbidden by the Church) were regarded as protection against evil. The sprite or elf personified the clinical symptom and the pentagram was an effective antidote.

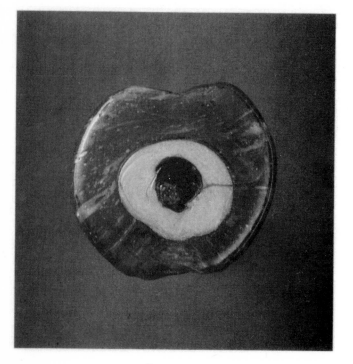

Eye amulet (apotropaion).
For protection against the evil eye bewitching and enchanting.
Asia Minor. Diameter 1¼ inches
Schweizerisches Pharmazie-
historisches Museum, Basle.
Photograph: P. Heman, Basle.

trahlungsgefäss or radiance
el.
rtz mounted in silver;
diance was supposed to afford
ection against eye complaints.
ht 8 ½ inches.
reizerisches Pharmazie-
risches Museum, Basle.
ograph: P. Heman, Basle.

Salerno

By the 9th and 10th centuries, the medical school at Salerno was famed throughout the West. Its geographical position just south of Naples favoured the development of *Civitas hippocratica*, as Salerno was later called. A mild climate and ancient tradition as a health resort encouraged the school to develop as a place of medical tuition. The Hellenic tradition had persisted here for longer than in the rest of western Europe and during the Crusades there was an active dialogue with the Levant which probably acted as a fresh stimulus to the physicians in Salerno. Unlike the ecclesiastical seats of learning, Salerno was a laical school, although its physicians remained on good terms with the clergy. There is even evidence that women were educated as physicians in Salerno.

Constantine the African, who was born in Carthage in about 1020, had a profound influence on the development of Salerno. For many years he travelled throughout the Near East as a drug merchant and with his alert mind and facility for languages he procured a thorough grounding in philosophy and medicine. In about 1060 he went to Italy, where he began work as a translator. He was the first to introduce Arab learning into the West. In 1076 he withdrew into the abbey of Monte Cassino where he found an understanding benefactor in the abbot Desiderius. Constantine died at Monte Cassino in 1087.

His work on Arabic, Greek and some Byzantine texts marked a new epoch in contemporary medicine. The work of Constantine greatly enhanced the reputation of the Salerno School which, within a few decades, was producing its own medical literature. Constantine's most important work was his Latin rendering of the writings of Ali Ibn Al-Abbas. Constantine called this *pantegni* (the entire art). He did not mention the name of the Arabian author, probably for political reasons. The Saracens were repeatedly making heavy raids on the coastal towns of Italy and so it would not have been expedient to publish the work of an Arabian scholar openly, at that moment.

Constantine's translations and compendia promulgated the basic learning of Hippocrates and Galen to mediaeval physicians and the documents opened up entirely new vistas of scientific thought. The famous dispensatories of the School of Salerno include Arabic drugs, and books on pharmacology were written for practical use.

The *Antidotarius magnus seu universalis* was produced shortly before A.D. 1100 by several Salerno physicians working in collaboration. In the first half of the 13th

Gold coin, Augustal.
Emperor Frederick II (1194–1250).
Struck in Brindisi or Messina
1231/1250.
Photograph:
Hirmer Fotoarchiv, Munich.

century, Master Nicholas incorporated the 115 most important formulae from the *Antidotarius magnus* in a compendium for practical use.

The *Dynameron* of Nikolaos Myrepsos, written in Greek, appeared in the first third of the 14th century. The author's name is not his own, but the Byzantine name for an apothecary.

Matthaeus Platearius was a prominent commentator of his period. He extended the pharmaceutical side of the *Antidotarium*, adding a detailed *materia medica* arranged in alphabetical order. This book, the title of which is taken from the first two words *Circa instans,* became renowned and was an important influence throughout the Middle Ages.

A dispensatory written in about 1490 by Nicole Prévost (Nicolaus Praepositus) in France is wrongly ascribed to the School of Salerno.

A didactic poem, *Regimen sanitatis salernitanum,* also became very widely known.

One of the most important lists of drugs from Salerno, the *Alphita,* includes vegetable drugs and also animal organs, animals, minerals, chemicals, pharmaceutical preparations and a list of terms commonly used in medical practice.

In 1231, Emperor Frederick von Hohenstaufen issued a medical decree in the Kingdom of Sicily. He directed that there should be a well-defined distinction between physicians and apothecaries. The candidates had to sit an examination in Salerno. Having passed, physicians had to do a year's practical training under the supervision of an experienced physician.

Frederick II's decree provided a standard for all subsequent medical legislation, including the Basle Apothecary's Oath. This was drawn up some time after 1271 and was the first apothecaries' charter in the German language.

'We, Thüring der Marschalch, Burgomaster, and the Council and the Guild Masters, have come to a unanimous agreement, having consulted the wishes and counsel of our Lord the Bishop and other honourable persons, that no physician who cares or has cared for the sick shall ever own an apothecary's business in Basle, nor shall he ever become an apothecary; and in Basle no one who tests the urine of the sick, or who is a physician shall own an apothecary's business; and if any physician who at present has an apothecary's business does not completely relinquish ownership of this business in the space of time allowed him, after that time he will have to pay, without fail, one mark of silver as often as medicine is seen in his room. And anyone who has, or who superintends an apothecary's business must swear a special oath each year to the new Council, that no physician owns any part or share of his business or of his medicines. And because we have learnt by experience that this is in the public interest, we desire that this arrangement shall be made absolutely permanent. We have also reached complete agreement as regards the oath, that before any man or woman shall ever again own an apothecary's business in Basle, and before anyone ever becomes an apothecary, he must convince the Council by his oath that he is worthy of the position in skill and knowledge and has practised for a sufficiently long time for people to be able to rely on him. Also, anyone who is or who becomes an apothecary in Basle must provide for each physician what he asks and demands, if there is anything which he has not got, he must state that he has not got it, and everything which he provides for the physician must be of such quality and of such usefulness that he knows, upon his oath, that it will be good and useful for the confection which the physician is making. The physician must not come to any (private) agreement with the apothecary about what he is taking to the sick person, unless the sick person's messenger is present. Remember also to include in the oath administered to the apothecaries that they shall not allow anyone to buy poison, unless the buyer has two guarantors who will guarantee that no one shall suffer harm from it.' The Oath is undated, but since it was issued at the time of Burgomaster Thüring Marschalk, who held office from 1271–1322, it must have been issued between these dates. Staatsarchiv, Basle. Photograph: P. Heman, Basle.

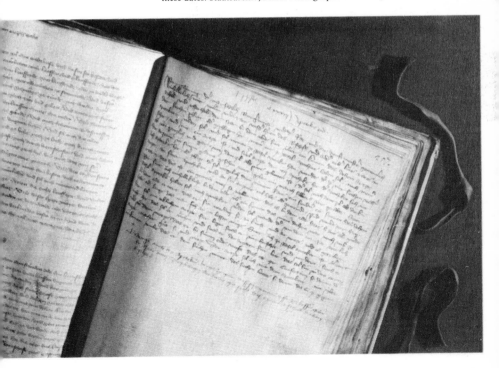

Fourteenth and fifteenth centuries

There were no major medical advances in the fourteenth and fifteenth centuries, a period in which people became obsessed with the Arabesque, that is to say, Arab knowledge in the guise of scholasticism. Few were prepared to question the authoritarian dogma of the time and, often enough, important advances such as distillation were used in practice but hushed up scientifically. In the universities, students often learnt practical medicine outside the scope of formal lectures. However, there was a gradual change and both natural scientists and theologians like William of Occam and Nicholas Cusanus encouraged an individu-

alistic approach to thought. Pietro de Abano (1250–1316) was one of the first physicians to criticize the rigid scholastic system.

Fourteenth-century Europe was ravaged by recurrent epidemics of plague, and an important advance at this time was the realization that Black Death was contagious. Admittedly there were no concrete ideas as to the cause or mode of dissemination of the disease, but many local authorities took steps to isolate the sick. In 1377, Ragusa issued the first quarantine order. For treatment, physicians prescribed fumigation, herb sachets and administration of

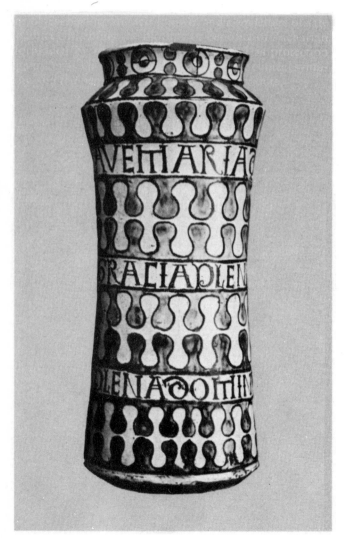

Albarello in Mozarabic style. Decorated in green and mangar contraposed wavy lines alterna with bands. In the bands is the lettering 'AVE MARIA GRACIA PI Aragon, 16th century.
Museo de la Farmacia Hispana Facultad de Farmacia, Madrid.

theriac. Guy de Chauliac, the great French surgeon (circa 1300–circa 1370), attempted to cure plague bubo with plasters of figs and pistachios.

An important step in the advancement of medicine was the study of anatomy and tutorial post mortems. Originally these were only used to confirm Galenic anatomy in the form handed down by the Arabs. Surgery threw off the shackles of tradition sooner than medicine. Ugo Borgognoni, a surgeon in Bologna who died in about 1258, recommended anaesthesia with 'sleeping sponges' before an operation. Sponges soaked in decoctions of opium, hyos-

cyamus, hemlock and other types of drug were tied in front of the patient's mouth and nose.

During these centuries there was an ominous belief in magic of all kinds and this eventually led to terrifying trials of persons suspected of witchcraft. Magic symbols, faith healing and sacred amulets became widely used to combat disease and many physicians included a number of the old animal remedies in their medicine chests. Blood, bile, bone and even the excrement of mammals, amphibians and reptiles were used externally and internally. A later development of this was organotherapy, based on the idea of re-

Albarello
Hispano-Moresque, decorated in gold and blue with metallic lustre
Paterna, 15th century.
Museo de la Farmacia Hispana, Facultad de Farmacia, Madrid.

placing a diseased by a healthy organ. For instance, the kidneys of goats and sheep were prescribed for kidney diseases.

Astrology was also a great influence on medicinal therapeutics and many a doctor of good repute styled himself *medicus astrologicus*.

In spite of the popularity of pseudo-sciences, there was unmistakable progress towards a healthy sense of reality. As more people became educated, the public at large became interested in medicine. University studies and examinations gave the physician a title, he commanded respect

emagne with the angel and the
Carlina acaulis. During one of
mpaigns, pestilence broke out
gst his army. The Emperor
d to God for assistance and an
is reputed to have appeared
old him that he must fire an
, which would then fall on a
This plant would halt the
e. The Emperor did as the angel
idden him and the arrow fell
histle. Ever since then the
has borne the name *Carlina*.
ture from Northern Italy,
f the 15th century.
ische Staatsbibliothek, Munich.
t researches suggest that the
depicted here is possibly not
emagne but St. Stephan of
ary.

and his contemporaries looked upon him with a certain amount of awe. As towns flourished, guilds became strictly organized and apothecaries and drug merchants united to form corporate bodies. We have evidence of this development in Verona as early as 1221.

The travels of Marco Polo (1254–1324) and other merchants were significant events in the annals of pharmacognosy. Drugs and spices had certainly reached Europe before the Portugese discovered the sea route to the Far East, but people only had a vague idea as to where and how these plants were cultivated. These travellers often reported on foreign cultivated plants, and a general interest in spices and drugs helped to extend the therapeutic armamentarium.

...rello.
...orated with horizontal rows of
...or ivy leaves, with the colour
...ging from leaf to leaf.
...ises, end of the 15th century.
...eo de la Farmacia Hispana,
...ltad de Farmacia, Madrid.

Renaissance

from the register of the Basle
ecary H. T. Eglinger
-1675).
eizerisches Pharmazie-
ches Museum, Basle.
graph: P. Heman, Basle.

The period which we refer to as the Renaissance did not immediately herald any startling innovations in medicine or pharmacy. The antiquarian tradition, Arabic ideas and folk medicine were firmly established modes of thought. After the fall of Constantinople (1453), the original Greek texts were brought to the West and translating them became a matter of philological medicine. The invention of printing resulted in a gradual dissemination of knowledge and education, but early printed books seldom contained contemporary work. They were nearly all books of ancient knowledge, such as traditional formulae and prescriptions.

One of the earliest printed books is an astrological calendar for blood-letting (1456). In spite of the trend towards enlightenment and humanism, science, folk medicine and superstition became even more closely allied.

Scientific thought was certainly not immune from the violent political and religious conflicts of the 16th century. Although scholasticism persisted, the humanistic ideas of the Renaissance gained in popularity. The Scientific Renaissance was not instigated by direct translations from the Greek; it stemmed from a rejection of rigid authoritarian belief. Experimentation and practical experience began to take precedence over theoretical learning. Paracelsus clearly indicated the way ahead, with his exhortation: *Perscrutamini naturas rerum.*

The voyages of Vasco da Gama and Bartolomeu Dias, and the discovery of America by Columbus in 1492, opened up new worlds and shattered belief in ancient traditions.

The obsession with alchemy gradually declined and was replaced by chemistry. Valerius Cordus (1515–1544) was the first to prepare sulphuric ether. There was an upsurge of interest in botany with all its pharmacotherapeutic implications. The work of the three scholars Otto Brunfels (1488–1534), Hieronymus Bock (1498–1554) and Leonhart

Florentine receiver.
This was used as a receiver in d[...]
tion, particularly for light and
heavy oils.
17th century. Height 9½ inche[...]
Schweizerisches Pharmazie-
historisches Museum, Basle.
Photograph: P.Heman, Basle.

Fuchs (1501–1566) prompted a re-evaluation of botany and they are regarded as the fathers of this science.

Brunfels was closely associated with the humanists. In 1524 he went to Strasbourg as a lecturer, where he devoted himself to the study of medicine and botany. His work was still to some extent influenced by Dioscorides and Pliny, but it contains a good deal of information about plants of the Strasbourg district. Woodcuts by the painter Hans Weydlitz in Brunfels' *Herbarium* are particularly valuable. The sketches for these were done under the direction of Brunfels himself.

In most of the older botanical books, the author left the illustrations entirely to the artist, who was often unfamiliar with the complete plant and so was inclined to exercise too much artistic licence in the drawing. In Brunfels' work, the plants are depicted with scientific accuracy. His main contribution to botany was his attempt to identify plants described by the ancients and to standardize the nomenclature.

Brunfels encouraged Hieronymus Bock to publish his work. Bock's descriptions, which are very accurate and based on personal observation, are almost exclusively of

Care of the sick.
Part of a terracotta relief depicti
Christian charity. Work of Santi
Viviani, between 1526 and 1528.
Pistoia, Ospedale del Ceppo.
Photograph: Studio Arborio Me
Milan.

oater.
s with hinged lid. The top half
e sphere bears a coat of arms.
century. Height 3½ inches.
/eizerisches Pharmazie-
risches Museum, Basle.
ograph: P. Heman, Basle.

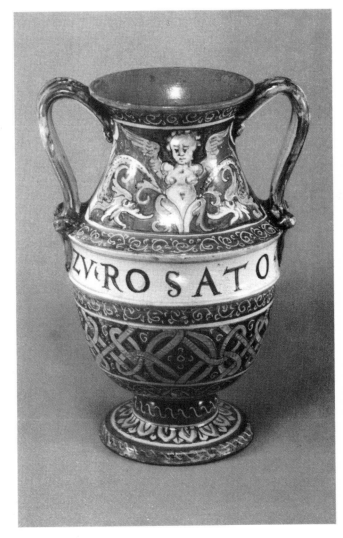

thecary's storage jar.
with handles and rich flame-
ured decoration. Lettering: Zu.
ato (Zucchero rosato).
na, 16th century.
lical history collection of
offmann-La Roche & Co. Ltd,
e.
tograph: P. Heman, Basle.

Apothecary's balance.
Bronze, gilded.
16th century, from Augsburg.
Height of balance with pedestal:
19 inches.
Schweizerisches Pharmazie-
historisches Museum, Basle.
Photograph: P. Heman, Basle.

indigenous plants. Among the remedies he mentions are a liquorice pastille, he recommends *Cydonia* for preparing poultices and *Radix gentianae* for dilating wounds.

At practically the same time as Bock, Leonhart Fuchs was engaged on a similar task. He was born near Nördlingen, studied at the University of Erfurt and later founded an academy in Wemding. In 1521 he became Magister at the University of Ingolstadt and in 1524 a Doctor of Medicine. When he died he was Professor at the University of Tübingen. The text of his major botanical book is excellent and it is beautifully illustrated, the figures and descriptions being juxtaposed. The German edition appeared in Basle in 1543 under the title *New Kräuterbuch*.

Unfortunately, no one would publish the best herbal of the 16th century and it did not appear until the middle of the 18th century. The author was Conrad Gesner, a learned scholar well versed in all the sciences, but who never achieved the recognition he deserved during his lifetime. He was born in 1516 and succumbed to the plague in 1565.

Dispensatoria and pharmacopoeias played an important part in the preparation and supply of drugs. Saladin of Ascoli's *Compendium aromatariorum* appeared in 1450 and represented a kind of pharmaceutical vademecum.

onstruction of an old pharmacy.
ately owned by Mr. and Mrs.
Schmid-Brunner, Diessenhofen.
tograph: U. Leibacher, Beringen,
tzerland.

Nicolaus Praepositus' *Dispensarium ad aromatarios* appeared in 1490 in Lyons. Praepositus, whose real name was Nicole Prévost, held practical knowledge in high esteem and part of his work deals with the preparation and storage of drugs.

In 1499, Lodovico Toscanelli in Florence published the *Nuovo Receptario*, which was written in Italian.

The city of Nuremberg commissioned the physician Valerius Cordus to compile an official dispensatory which appeared in 1546, shortly after the death of the author, under the title *Pharmacorum conficiendorum ratio Vulgo*

Set of weights.
Bronze. Sea-horse and mermaids c
the lid. The fastening is in the shap
of two horses' heads. Nested weigh
Dated 1616. Height 4 inches.
Schweizerisches Pharmazie-
historisches Museum, Basle.
Photograph: P. Heman, Basle.

Memento-mori pendant.

Death's head, silver, partially gilded pendant. Pomander for warding off the plague, with partitioned containers for medicaments and scented sponges.

16th or 17th century. Height 1 inch.

Historisches Museum, Basle.

Photograph: P. Heman, Basle.

Alchemist of the Late Middle Ages preparing guaiacum wood. This drug was commonly used to treat syphilis in the 16th century.

Title woodcut from Ulrich von Hutten's book *Von der wunderbarlichen Artzney des holtz Guaiacum.*

Strasbourg 1519.

Bilderarchiv Ciba, Basle.

vocant dispensatorium. In 1567, Florence followed the example of Nuremberg with the *Ricettario fiorentino.*

The word *pharmacopoeia* also appeared at about this time. Jacques Dubois (Jacobus Sylvius), Professor of Medicine in Paris, used the title *Pharmakopoe* for his formulary published in 1548 in Lyons.

Cordus was born in 1515 and his father was Professor of Medicine in Marburg. Cordus travelled a good deal and he was an acute observer of nature. He died in Rome in 1544. Conrad Gesner unselfishly published his work posthumously. We can see from his books that Cordus was not only an outstanding botanist, but also a mineralogist and chemist and he was a great innovator on every front. He described the preparation of extracts from *Helleborus niger,* rhubarb and aloes, and the preparation of essential oils. Cordus gives us a detailed description of the preparation and rectification of sulphuric acid.

After the discovery of America, many new and hitherto unknown drugs were brought to Europe. Among the best known were balsam of Peru, elemi, ipecacuanha, sarsaparilla, coca, hamamelis, tobacco, guaiacum wood, sassafras, condurango, cinchona bark, capsicum and vanilla.

The introduction of guaiacum wood, also known as *lignum sanctum,*caused a great stir at the beginning of the 16th century because it was reputed to be effective against syphilis, which had long been endemic. Many pamphlets were distributed about the wonder drug, the most famous of these being that of Ulrich von Hutten. This pamphlet, written in 1518, bore the title: *Ulrici de Hutten, Eq. De Guaiaci medicina et morbo gallico liber unus.*

The title page of the German edition (Strasbourg 1519) depicts a guaiacum vendor with a physician and two patients seated at his table.

rading sign of a *Löwenapotheke*
(lion' pharmacy) from Canton
Thurgau.
Carved from soft wood, painted
with gold and silver. The pedestal
has been renewed.
Height 16½ inches.
Kunsthaus Lempertz, Cologne.

Terra sigillata

Sealed earth was a mineral which had been used medicinally for centuries. It was first employed on the island of Lemnos where it was used to treat the foetid wounds of Philoctetes, one of the heroes of the Trojan War. In classical times there was a shrine of Aesculapius on the island and the priestess of this shrine had the exclusive right to work the clay. She did this whilst performing special rites and then distributed it amongst the sick. To prevent fraud, the clay tablets were stamped with a seal (terra sigillata). Philoctetes is depicted on one of the Lemnos tablets.

In Roman times, sealed earth from Arezzo was highly

rra sigillata.
om Lemnos, depicting Philoctetes.
ntiquity. Diameter ½ inch.
hweizerisches Pharmazie-
storisches Museum, Basle.
otograph: P. Heman, Basle.

valued. It was used to make medicinal pastilles and also for vessels which were decorated in relief.

In the Middle Ages and until fairly recently, white clay from the Milk Grotto in Bethlehem was highly prized. Women who were having difficulty in breast-feeding used this miraculous drug, called 'Mary's milk', in the hope that it would increase the flow of milk. Sealed earth was also thought to be effective against plague and it was in great demand during major epidemics. This meant that there was a constant search for fresh sources of supply and the medicinal clay was discovered in Sienna, on Malta, in Hungary, France and Silesia. *Terra miraculosa*, found in Saxony at the end of the 16th century, became extremely popular. Drinking vessels were also made from this and it was said that anyone drinking from these would be immune from any kind of poisoning. Water kept in these vessels was used as a remedy for snake-bites.

Terra sigillata rubra.
Silesia. Diameter 1 inch.
Schweizerisches Pharmazie-
historisches Museum, Basle.
Photograph: P. Heman, Basle.

Terra sigillata rubra.
From Eisleben, stamped with cres
and coat of arms.
Diameter 1½ inches.
Schweizerisches Pharmazie-
historisches Museum, Basle.
Photograph: P. Heman, Basle.

ling vessel of red terra sigillata.
sia. Height 3¾ inches.
weizerisches Pharmazie-
orisches Museum, Basle.
tograph: P. Heman, Basle.

Paracelsus

We can justifiably call Paracelsus the reformer of medicine. Veneration and hatred have distorted his historical character, but it is important to try to understand him and his work in the context of his time.

Theophrastus of Hohenheim was born in Einsiedeln in 1493, son of physician Wilhelm Bombast of Hohenheim, and he adopted the name Paracelsus later. He was still young when he began to travel widely, visiting universities in many countries, and he graduated Doctor of Medicine in Ferrara. On his travels he was an avid seeker after knowledge and learning from every possible source, from farm-

page of a book by Paracelsus
t medicine, treatment of wounds
drugs.
ished by Adam von Bodenstein.
ed in Frankfort-on-Main, 1566.
othek des Schweizerischen
mazie-historischen Museums,
e.
ograph: P. Heman, Basle.

ers, shepherds, ore miners or whoever he met. In 1526 he went to Basle where he became municipal medical officer but, six months later, disputes with authority forced him to flee the city. Paracelsus then began a wandering life of deprivation through Germany, Switzerland and Austria until he died in Salzburg in 1541.

Paracelsus' greatest achievement was to put chemistry at the service of medicine. His teaching, later called iatro-chemistry, was based on the notion that 'it is the task of chemistry to produce medicines for the treatment of disease, since the vital functions of life are basically chemical in nature'. This new idea consciously opposed alchemy, and directly opposed the older systems like those of Galen and the Arabs. Paracelsus did not attack the actual drugs so much as the complicated formulation of medicines of the old dispensatoria. He still used many medicinal herbs, but he believed that they should act on their own, without being mixed together. Another of his ideas was that if there is a disease, there must be a drug to treat it. Paracelsus was a Neoplatonist who was greatly influenced by mysticism. His concept of drug action was based on the idea that 'the actual essence of things is not in substances themselves but in the archeus within them, a force derived from God, also called the *quinta essentia,* which stimulates the other forces'. He tried to concentrate this vital force by chemical means. Paracelsus introduced the idea of extracting the active principle from a crude drug, and he was the true founder of pharmaceutical chemistry.

As a mystic he believed in the doctrine of a constant analogy between the microcosm and macrocosm and in the mutual interactions between stars, atmosphere and disease. Paracelsus defined five *entia* or influences which produce disease: *ens astrorum* (cosmic influence), *ens veneni* (influence of poisons), *ens naturale* (hereditary predisposition), *ens spirituale* (mental disorders) and *ens deale* (divine

nulary of Philippine Welser.
mulae were collected by physi-
s and apothecaries, and also by
ole interested in medicine.
ippine Welser's vast collection of
rulae has been preserved from
rime of Paracelsus. This valuable
nuscript provides us with informa-
about folk medicine and medical
erstition of the 16th century.
ippine Welser (1527–1580) was
ghter of the famous Augsburg
ily, the Welsers. In 1557 she
ried Archduke Ferdinand of Tirol,
n of Emperor Ferdinand I. She
le her collection of formulae
lst she was Mistress of Schloss
bras near Innsbruck.

formula illustrated reads as
ows:

aukrafft waser zou ainer mas
il.
t rerla
t negla
t mustgatnus
andfol kolrosen
andfol weysrosen
ndfol lavandelblanta
ndfol yosoptla
ndfol majoran
galgat
un gestoss gwirtz sol ma stosen
lein das alles zu samen geden
den besen mas wein das gschit
also wol vermacht 9 oder 10 dag
n sten dar nach aus gebrent.

orant water to make up to one
s (about 1.6 to 1.8 litres).
ts stick cinnamon (1 lot was about
rams)
ts cloves
ts nutmeg
andfuls peonies
andfuls white roses
ndfuls lavender blossom
ndfuls hyssop
andful marjoram
(dram) galingale
uncrushed spices are to be
hed, but not too fine, and all
ed together, and also the besen
old measure of quantity) of wine.
s is to be shaken until well mixed,
wed to stand for 9 or 10 days,
then distilled.

sthistorisches Museum, Schloss
bras collections, Innsbruck.
tograph: A. Demanega, Inns-
ck.

providence). Drugs were supposed to enhance the archeus and so eliminate the root cause of the disease.

Paracelsus also believed in, and was an enthusiastic advocate of the doctrine of 'signatures'. The doctrine of 'signatures', which had been handed down from Antiquity, was based on the idea that appearance and colour is the most perfect expression of function. Applying this to plants, it meant that the therapeutic effect of a plant could be predicted from its external appearance. This was one of the basic ideas behind the theory of 'signatures' and we can do no more than touch on the profound effect it had

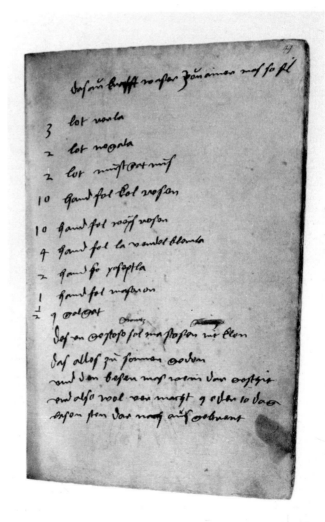

on the thinking of Paracelsus. He himself summarized the theory as follows: 'Everything born of Nature is fashioned to reveal its intrinsic properties.' Consequently, plants with heart-shaped leaves would be effective against heart disease, thistles against stabbing pain, etc.

Paracelsus was often abusive and vehement and this made him many enemies, but he fought to uphold his convictions. The physician's work was his greatest concern and he regarded *virtus* as one of the four pillars of medicine.

Paracelsus said: 'A physician develops from the heart,

Description and illustration of the apple-tree. Page from a herbal by P. A. Mathiolus, enlarged by J. Camerarius, 1590.
Bibliothek des Schweizerischen Pharmazie-historischen Museum Basle.
Photograph: P. Heman, Basle.

he is a product of the Almighty and his being is of the natural light, experience.'

'The pinnacle of medicine is love.'

Description and illustration of the pistachio bush (bladder nut). From a herbal by P. A. Mathiolus, enlarged by J. Camerarius, 1590. Bibliothek des Schweizerischen Pharmazie-historischen Museums, Basle. Photograph: P. Heman, Basle.

Healing vessels

Naturally enough, drug jars for storing medicaments were widely used, but healing vessels were also of importance. It was believed that special ingredients were produced in the healing vessel or that the vessel imparted to its contents a fluid which enhanced the curative action. Other vessels were used for testing the contents for poisonous agents. Amongst primitive races, the skull of a slain enemy was used for a similar purpose, as the virtues of the vanquished were supposed to be passed on to the conqueror. In the West, rare objects from far off countries were particularly prized, and precious stones, ostrich eggs, corals and animal

l-oyster shell engraved with
vity scene. The shell was used as
aling vessel.
hern France, 18th century.
ght 4 inches.
veizerisches Pharmazie-
orisches Museum, Basle.
tograph: P. Heman, Basle.

horns were widely used. The most famous horn used to make healing vessels was that of the fabulous unicorn. Two commercial forms, *unicornu marinum* and *fossile,* were sold in pharmacies.

Goblets and spoons for testing medicaments were made of unicorn and it was claimed that they sweated when brought into contact with poison. The crude drug unicorn was usually narwhal tusk.

The tortoise was a symbol of fertility and longevity. The shell and flesh of the animal were prized as tonics, and healing vessels of tortoise-shell were very costly.

Folding wooden medicine spoon
With carving of Saint George.
Length 6¼ inches.
Schweizerisches Pharmazie-
historisches Museum, Basle.
Photograph: P. Heman, Basle.

Mother-of-pearl shells were supposed to be 'diaphoretic' and 'to strengthen the heart', and mystic or religious symbols were often engraved on shells to enhance their healing effect.

Quartz was reputed to be effective against eye disorders, scrofula and cardiac and gastric disorders. Aristotle recommended it for dropsy and the crystal was used for centuries for making testing goblets.

The reputed curative properties of gold and silver as *aurum* and *argentum potabile* were one of the legacies of alchemy.

ver medicine goblet.
eight 3 inches.
hweizerisches Pharmazie-
storisches Museum, Basle.
otograph: P. Heman, Basle.

According to Lonitzer, who died in 1586, 'gold strengthens the heart, restores the blood and cures leprous conditions and scab'.

Medicine bottle bearing the pictu[re] of a saint.
Southern German, circa 1760.
Height 5 ½ inches.
Collection of Dr. H. Schmid-Brunn[er]
Diessenhofen.
Photograph: P. Heman, Basle.

Tortoise-shell used as a medicine goblet.
The tortoise was a symbol of fertility and longevity. Silver moun[t]ing, gilded.
17th century. Height 6 ½ inches.
Schweizerisches Pharmazie-historisches Museum, Basle.
Photograph: P. Heman, Basle.

ling vessel made from terra
[si]llata. Silesia. Height 4½ inches.
[Sch]weizerisches Pharmazie-
[hist]orisches Museum, Basle.
[Phot]ograph: P.Heman, Basle.

The dragonstone of Lucerne

The district around the Pilatus mountain in Switzerland is rich in fables and legends. The spirit of Pilatus, governor of the province, is said to have been banished to a small lake in the main group of mountains, and other tales tell of monsters and dragons. The old name for Pilatus, *Fräckmünt* or *Fractum montem*, describes the rugged shape of the mountain. Skeletons of extinct monsters have been discovered in the caves known as dragons' dens, and these were thought to be the bones of dragons. The history of the Lucerne dragonstone gives us a very interesting insight into the folk medicine of past centuries. Johann Leopold

Cysat (1601–1663), grandson of the chronicler and town apothecary Renward Cysat, wrote in some detail about this stone in his *Beschreibung dess berühmbten Lucerner- oder 4 Waldstättersees.*

Martin Schryber (1476–1531), clerk of the court and surgeon in Lucerne, had an insolvent debtor, the Rothenburg farmer Rudolf Stempflin, who owned the precious dragonstone. Stempflin described to Schryber, the surgeon, how one day a fiery dragon had flown from Rigi towards Pilatus and brushed past him. He was dazed for a moment or two, but when he recovered he found the dragonstone on the ground in a clot of blood. The curative power of this round stone in cases of haemorrhage and poisoning bordered on the miraculous and so Stempflin had never sold it, even though he had been offered a great deal of money for it. However, the farmer was persistently in Schryber's debt, and finally a court of law awarded the surgeon the stone in lieu of payment.

In the year of the plague, 1519, the *Pestkugel* as the dragonstone was also known, proved its magical powers. In 1523, Schryber had a commission from the town of Lucerne officially confirm the curative powers of the stone, and over the years it must have brought this enterprising physician many a handsome fee.

In the course of time, physicians and scholars studied the dragonstone, and Felix Platter, a friend of Renward Cysat, cast doubt on its power to heal. Johann Jakob Scheuchzer (1672–1733) called the stone a 'rare and precious wonder of nature'. It appears on Scheuchzer's map of Switzerland of 1712 as one of the great rarities of the country. On the other hand, the prominent physician and natural scientist Moritz Anton Kappeler (1685–1768) was very amused by its alleged magic powers and by the history of the stone. Research workers of the 19th century believed the stone to be an artificially coloured meteorite and in 1860 August Feierabend from Lucerne states that, on the basis of its specific gravity, the stone could be fired clay. Since the dragonstone must not be damaged, it is difficult to find out any more about it. In any case, the surface may be artificial.

The famous dragonstone has now served its purpose as a stone with curative and miraculous powers, and the Schweizerisches Pharmazie-historisches Museum in Basle now have it on loan from the Historisches Museum, Lucerne.

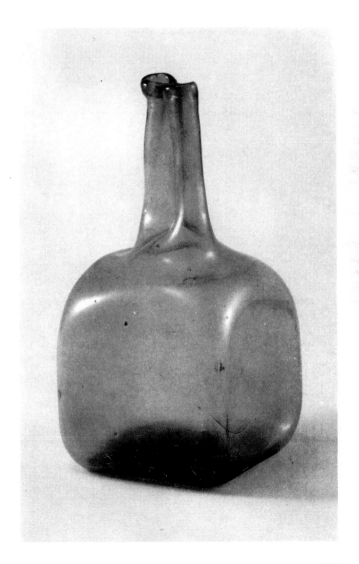

are bottle with a double neck.
century. Height 9 inches.
weizerisches Pharmazie-
orisches Museum, Basle.
tograph: P. Heman, Basle.

Seventeenth and eighteenth centuries

The ideas of Paracelsus and the pioneer work done by anatomist Andreas Vesal (1515–1564) were a great stimulus to scholars of the 17th century, and the 17th and 18th centuries saw the scientific exploitation of pharmacology and medicinal therapeutics.

Johann Baptist van Helmont (1577–1644), who was still influenced by Paracelsian ideas, recommended the introduction of many chemical substances into *materia medica* and he developed a number of methods for preparing chemical compounds. Helmont introduced the term 'gas' and he discovered carbonic acid.

It was François de la Boë Sylvius who really adopted the chemical concepts of Paracelsus and applied them to therapeutics. De la Boë Sylvius' theory was that diseases were due either to 'acid acrimony' or 'alkaline acrimony' and in either case treatment consisted of redressing the chemical balance.

Sylvius was born in 1614 in Hanau, the son of an emigrant Dutch nobleman. He studied at a number of universities, later practised in Hanau and Amsterdam and eventually accepted a teaching post in the University of Leyden. He died in Leyden in 1672.

A plague-physician's apparel during the plague epidemic in Marseilles, 1790.
Editions Rencontre, Lausanne.
Photograph: N. Bouvier, Geneva, and R. J. Segalat, Paris.

Physician Johann Rudolf Glauber (1604–1668) was born in Karlstadt (Franconia). He worked in Salzburg, Frankfort-on-Main, Cologne and Amsterdam and died in Amsterdam in 1668. He was an alchemist bent on preparing medicinal arcana, but his studies on the decomposition of salts by acids and bases represent important milestones in the development of chemistry. Crystalline sodium sulphate is called Glauber's salt after him.

The flow of new crude drugs from the New World continued on into the 17th century. In the 1640's, cinchona bark was introduced for treating malaria. Jesuit priests were

oles cupboard from the Delft
egium Pharmaceuticum. The
oard holds a complete miniature
macy with drug jars and phials
e of Delft ware. Dated 1730.
ht 83 inches; depth 37 inches;
dth 28½ inches.
smuseum, Amsterdam.
ograph: Rijksmuseum,
terdam.

mainly responsible for making this most important drug known in Europe and there is a charming legend associated with the name cinchona. The story goes that the wife of a Spanish Viceroy in Peru, the Countess of Chinchón, was cured of malaria by cinchona bark. The drug then came on to the market in Europe as countess powder or Jesuit's powder and Linnaeus was the first to call the bark 'cinchona' in honour of the Countess of Chinchón.

As more drugs were discovered, the volume of pharmacognostical literature grew. The *Pharmakopoea medicophysica* of the Frankfort municipal physician Johann-

'Anatomy' of a pharmacist.
French cartoon (N. Larmessin).
17th century.

Christian Schröder first appeared in 1641 in Ulm and this was to become one of the most famous pharmacopoeias of its time. Nicolas Lémery's *Dictionnaire universel des drogues simples* was published in Paris in 1698. The *Histoire générale des drogues* by pharmacist Pierre Pomet (Paris 1691) contains a list of all the drugs which he used and collected from the Jardin des Plantes. The work of the Basle physician and botanist Caspar Bauhin (1550–1624) subsequently became important for identifying vegetable *materia medica*.

In an attempt to learn more about medicinal plants,

ft ware jug for oil.
e specimen cylindrical in shape.
a rule, jugs for oils and syrups
e big-bellied.
rmaziehistorisches Museum,
sterdam.
tograph: Stedelijk Museum,
sterdam.

many universities established botanical gardens, parts of which were used exclusively for growing medicinal herbs.

Eighteenth-century philosophy, with its rejection of mysticism, had a palpable effect on the natural sciences. The phlogiston theory of the physician Ernst Stahl had some repercussions on the science of chemistry. This theory was based on the notion that bodies burned because of their phlogiston content. Oxygen had not yet been discovered, but Stahl had anticipated it.

Friedrich Hoffmann (1660–1742) was one of the most eminent pharmaceutical chemists of his time. He studied the essential oils, treated a number of them with reagents, e.g. nitric acid, and examined a number of drugs derived from animals and plants. In a discourse in 1718, Hermann Boerhaave (1668–1738), the Dutch Professor of Medicine, Chemistry and Botany in Leyden, outlined his attitude to contemporary problems in chemistry. He did not accept the phlogiston theory in full, but he believed that there is a life-giving substance in the atmosphere, because a lack of air causes death.

Robert Boyle (1627–1691), who was pre-eminent amongst all his predecessors and contemporaries, was the founder of modern analytical chemistry. He also made a detailed study of the process of combustion and discovered that combustion will not occur in a vacuum. His contributions to medicine and pharmacy included studies on, and improvements in the techniques for preparing pharmaco-chemicals.

As a result of his experiments on the effect of alcohol, silver nitrate, antimony chloride, etc. on animal tissues, Albrecht von Haller formulated his theory of muscle excitability and this theory had some repercussions on medicinal therapeutics. The contrastimulant theory of Giovanni Rasori (1766–1837) was influenced by the work of Haller. Rasori also noted that observation of the effects of a drug may help towards diagnosis.

Haller's botanical work was also of pharmacological significance. In 1776, Vicat (1720–1783), a physician from Lausanne, published an extract from Haller's botanical works under the title *La matière médicale tirée de Halleri stirpium helvetiae*. Hahnemann, the founder of homeopathy, translated Vicat's extract into German, under the title *Albrecht von Hallers Arzneimittellehre*. Haller's preface to the *Pharmakopoae Helvetica* 1771 is famous.

Albrecht von Haller was born in 1708 in Berne. After studying for short time in Tübingen he went to Leyden, where he attended lectures by Boerhaave. He graduated as

Simple microscope made of silver A. van Leeuwenhoek. Circa 1673. 1 × 1¾ inches; length of handle 1 inch.
Deutsches Museum, Munich.
Photograph: Lichtbildstelle, Deutsches Museum, Munich.

er medallion, Leipzig, 1700.
Johann Kittel. *Aloe americana*
oming for the first time in the
anius Gardens. Inscription:
oen Americ. annor. 28 altam Ped.
Ramis 35 Fl. protrudere 5138.
siae vidit Hortus Bosianus
OCC).' On the leaves:
tore E: Pein'.
the Bosanius Gardens in Leipzig
Aloe americana plant was
years old and 24 feet high, and
duced 5138 flowers on 35
nches. 1700.)

verse: view of Leipzig with the
sanius Gardens in the foreground.
cription: 'Sic Lipsia floreat usque'.
meter 1½ inches.
llection of Dr. A. Lutz, Basle.
otograph: P. Heman, Basle.

Doctor of Medicine when only 19 years of age. On journeys abroad he derived a great deal of intellectual stimulus from meeting many different scholars. At the age of 26 he was appointed Lecturer in Anatomy and director of a hospital by the City of Berne. Two years later, in 1736, he was invited to teach at the University of Göttingen and soon afterwards he became internationally renowned, with students from every country visiting Göttingen to hear him lecture. In 1753 he returned to Berne, but his home town did not grant him the recognition he deserved and he had to be content with the post of a second-rank official. He died in 1777.

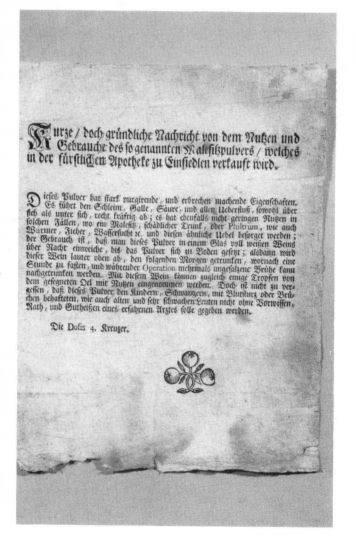

Recommendation for a *Malefiz* powder which was sold by the pharmacy of the monastery of Einsiedeln. End of the 18th century. Collection of Dr. E. Müller, Beromünster.
Photograph: P. Heman, Basle.

1785 saw the publishing of the book *An Account of the foxglove and some of its Medical Uses,* by the English physician William Withering. In this book, Withering advocated the therapeutic use of *Digitalis purpurea.* This recommendation was based on ten years' experience. By and large, the principles laid down by Withering for using digitalis are still valid today.

The work of Carl Wilhelm Scheele (1742–1786) heralded a new era in pharmaceutical chemistry. His work was aimed at purifying the active principle of a crude drug by crystallization, and he met with great success. His dis-

anter.
ysanthemum decoration.
ering: A.Buglossi.
nce, Paris or St-Cloud.
t half of the 18th century.
ght 11 inches.
weizerisches Pharmazie-
orisches Museum, Basle.
tograph: P.Heman, Basle.

coveries included glycerin, hydrocyanic acid and malic acid. His work surpassed anything that had been achieved before him in the field of phytochemical research. Between 1774 and 1775 he carried out experiments which led to an extremely important discovery, that of oxygen.

Carl Wilhelm Scheele was born in Stralsund in 1742. In 1757 he was apprenticed to a Göteborg pharmacist, where he completed his training as a self-educated chemist. In 1768 he started work in a pharmacy in Stockholm. His acquaintance with many distinguished scholars encouraged him to continue his studies and he read his first scien-

Apothecary's showpiece.
Wooden panel, with a raised desig
composed of mussel shells, snail
shells and coral branches depicting
sea-monster, from the old pharma
which served the Prince-arch-
bishop's court in Salzburg.
9 × 7 ½ inches. Probably 17th centu
Owned and photographed by the
Carolino Augusteum Museum,
Salzburg.

...tuary moulds.
...e moulds date back to the middle
...he 17th or beginning of the 18th
...tury. Some were prepared for
...rg Winckhler (1605–1667),
...prietor of the municipal phar-
...y, Innsbruck. The moulds were
...d for electuaries or confections.
...electuary is a thickened,
...etened fruit *purée* containing
...verized drugs (e.g. *Electuarium
...nae)*. In the possession of
...Franz Winkler, pharmacist,
...sbruck.
...tograph: Atelier Gasser,
...sbruck.

tific paper in the Stockholm Academy, to which he was elected as a member in 1775. In the same year he went to Köping to manage a pharmacy. Scheele remained in this small pharmacy, completely devoted to his chemical studies which took up a large proportion of his income. He carried on his work under the most difficult conditions imaginable and he was granted a stipend by the Academy. Scheele died at the age of 44, and Tschirch called him 'a born chemist'. The hand of Carl Wilhelm Scheele guided pharmaceutical chemistry into a new era.

Wet drug jar known as *chevrette*.
Manganese decoration.
Lettering: Syr. Capil. Vener.
Work of Luigi Levantino,
circa 1715, Savona.
Schweizerisches Pharmazie-
historisches Museum, Basle.
Photograph: P. Heman, Basle.

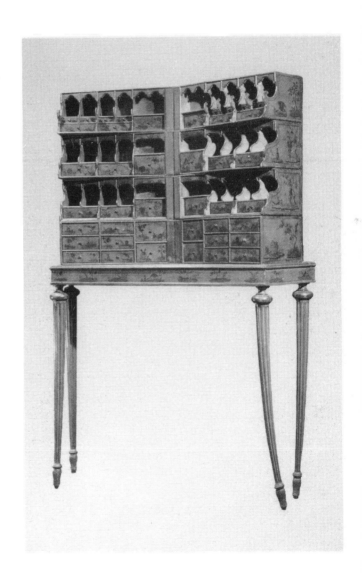

etian medicine chest.
century.
ght of table: 34 inches.
ght of superstructure: 26 inches.
gth of table: 44 inches.
th of superstructure: 18 inches.
uto di Storia della Medicina
 Università di Roma, Rome.
tograph: Mauro Pucciarelli,
ne.

Oil painting depicting medicinal herbs.
In the top centre of the picture, Christ is portrayed as a physician. The pictures show the following plants and symbols, starting from the top left:

1st row: Cowslip *(Primula officinalis* L.).
Globe as an imperial orb, symbol of the Holy Roman Empire.
Amaranthus caudatus L.
Figure symbolizing medicine.
Heath speedwell *(Veronica officinalis* L.).
Chicory *(Cichorium intybus* L.).

2nd row: Costmary *(Impatiens balsamina* L.).
Devilsbit scabious *(Succisa pratensis* L.).
Hemlock *(Conium maculatum* L.).
Castor-oil plant *(Ricinus communis* L.).
Egyptian fig-tree *(Ficus sycomorus* L.).
Crosswort gentian *(Gentiana cruciata* L.).

3rd row: Crucifix.
Herb Robert *(Geranium robertianum* L.).
Borage *(Borago officinalis* L.).
Pellitory of the wall *(Parietaria officinalis* L.).
Wall germander *(Teucrium chamaedrys* L.).
Ground-pine *(Ajuga chamaepitys).*

4th row: Turkscap lily *(Lilium martagon).*
Amulet, white pearls in a gold setting, to ease the pain of childbirth.
Pendant amulet with red stone.
Water forget-me-not *(Myosotis palustris).*
Verschreiherz for the protection of spirits.
Marjoram *(Origanum vulgare* L.).

This Baroque panel cannot be dated accurately. The artist did not work from nature, but copied the plants from herbals.
Size: 32 × 25 inches.
Germanisches Nationalmuseum, Nuremberg.

Application of these plants in folk medicine.
Primula officinalis: for gout, paralysis, coughing and as a cosmetic. Also, based on the theory of 'signatures', for treating jaundice.
Amaranthus caudatus: for dysentery, haematemesis and haematuria.
Veronica officinalis: for bladder disorders and bronchial catarrh.
Cichorium intybus: internally for urine and liver disorders, externally for abscesses.
Impatiens balsamina: for cleansing wounds.
Succisa pratensis: many uses.
Conium maculatum: externally for cooling in cases of erysipelas, resolvent for indurative ulcers.
Ricinus communis: purgative, and to stimulate hair growth.
Ficus sycomorus: purgative.
Gentiana cruciata: was popularly known as *Heil aller Schäden* (the 'cure-all').
Geranium robertianum: haemostatic.
Borago officinalis: cardiac stimulant.
Ajuga chamaepitys: for apoplexy, vertigo and gout; also used as an antitoxin.
Lilium martagon: the root is used for haemorrhoids and bladder disorders.
Myosotis palustris: according to the theory of 'signatures', it was good for the eyes.
Origanum vulgare: for gallbladder disease and dropsy.

Samuel Hahnemann

Up to the end of the 18th and beginning of the 19th century, advances and discoveries such as those of Boerhaave and Scheele had found very little practical application in medicine. A number of systems were taught in medical schools, but students would not have found them very informative. There was still great emphasis on the use of drastic remedies such as purgatives and emetics, factual knowledge about medicines tended to be ignored by most physicians and pharmacists, and the complications of polypharmacy were still widely accepted and applied. Hahnemann's theories completely contradicted orthodox views and they

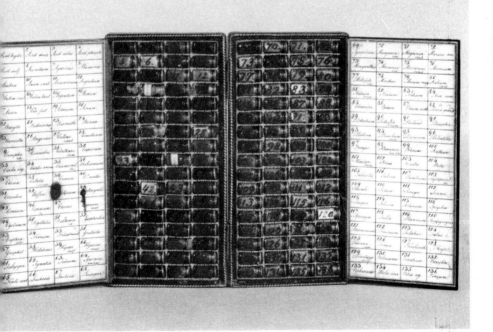

sparked off a bitter conflict between the advocates and opponents of his ideas. Probably Hahnemann's great contribution to medicine was in prompting the medical professions to investigate and test many of the medicaments they used, where this had not been done before. Even his opponents had to pay heed to his theories, if only to discount them.

Samuel Hahnemann was born in Meissen in 1755, son of a painter of porcelain. After completing his medical studies he worked as a physician in a number of places, but found the life dissatisfying and so turned his attention to science. He did a great deal of work in the field of pharmaceutical chemistry and this gave him a basic understanding of the nature of many drugs. A study by Cullen on cinchona bark prompted Hahnemann to try out this drug on himself. It gave him bouts of fever (probably because he was hypersensitive to it) and this led him to formulate his theory on the use of medicines. Hahnemann's method was based on the 'simile' principle which he summarized as: *similia similibus curantur*. The idea was to use extremely low doses of a drug to incite in the healthy person symptoms similar to those caused by the disease itself, the aim being to mobilize and redirect the vital forces in the body. He also

Apothecaries' weights.
Top: ounce and drachm weights.
Bottom: scruple, obolus and grain weights. The unit of weight on the old apothecary system (troy weight) was the pound (libra), which weighed somewhere between 380 and 500 g according to the region. The pound was divided into 12 ounces;
the ounce (onzia) into 8 drachms;
the drachm (drachma) into three scruples or two oboli;
the scruple (scrupulum) into 20 grains;
the grain (granum) weighed about 0.06 g.
The pound and half-pound were in the shape of a truncated pyramid, the ounce and drachm were zig-zag, the scruple and obolus were made of small brass rings and the grain weights of brass-plate.
Germanisches Nationalmuseum, Nuremberg.

insisted that medicinal treatment should be adapted to suit each case individually. He called his theory homeopathy (from the Greek homoios = similar), in contrast to allopathy, in which drugs are prescribed according to the principle of opposites: *contraria contrariis*.

Hahnemann also actively opposed the use of pharmaceutical mixtures so common in his time. He insisted that only one drug be used at a time so that its action could be observed in detail.

He called his technique of diluting drugs 'potentiation', and the procedure was as follows: first a strong alcoholic extract was prepared and then two drops of this primary tincture were diluted with 98 drops of spirit and the solution shaken vigorously. A drop of this solution was then taken and diluted with 99 drops of spirit. This process could be repeated up to 30 times, depending on the drug.

Hahnemann was quite fanatical in defending his ideas and he made plenty of enemies. Undoubtedly his theories had many advantages over the drastic methods in common use at the time, but Hahnemann did a great disservice to himself by being so dogmatic about them. Also, his theories were often misunderstood and hence vulnerable to charlatan exploitation.

all drug jar.
corated in polychrome.
tering: P. Lap. Smaragd. P.
gian
ft imitation, first half of the
h century.
ight 6 inches.
weizerisches Pharmazie-
torisches Museum, Basle.
otograph: P. Heman, Basle.

e Gaper, wood carving.
m the 16th century on, the gaper
s the trademark of Dutch
rmacies and chemists' shops.
pers were found mainly in
sterdam and occasionally in
nders.
rmaziehistorisches Museum,
sterdam.
otograph: Stedelijk Museum,
sterdam.

His most important publications were *Organon der rationellen Heilkunde,* published in 1810, *Reine Arzneimittellehre in sechs Teilen,* which appeared between 1811 and 1820, and the book *Die chronischen Krankheiten, ihre eigentümliche Natur und homöopathische Heilung,* published in 1828.

After publication of his *Organon,* Hahnemann began practice in Leipzig where he enjoyed popular acclaim, but professional enmity forced him to move his practice to Cöthen in 1821. In 1834 he went to Paris, where he died in 1843 after a stormy life often of great privation.

The dispute between homeopaths and allopaths. Death hovers over both of them, the inscription on his scythe reads: 'there is no herb growing that will prevent death'. Cartoon by Dürr, Berne, 1842. 11¼ × 14¾ inches. Schweizerisches Pharmazie-historisches Museum, Basle. Photograph: P. Heman, Basle.

Bottle plait with medicine bottles. This was how the pedlars brought medicine bottles made of Bohemian glass to the pharmacist.

The plait in the illustration dates back to the first half of the 18th century. Length 24 inches.

Collection of Dr. H. Schmid-Brunner, Riessenhofen.

Photograph: P. Heman, Basle.

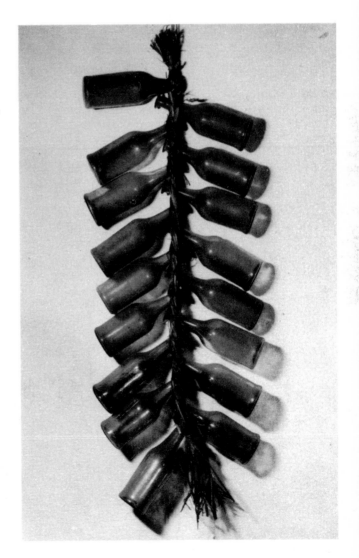

Nineteenth century

During the early part of the 19th century, the philosophy
of natural science became less and less empirical, and botany, zoology, chemistry and physics became integral parts
of medicine and pharmacy. The realization of the significance of the plant cell by botanist Matthias Jakob Schleiden (1804–1881) had vital implications for medicine, and
the discovery of microscopic species of fungi subsequently
formed the basis of the parasite theory. Schleiden's results
stimulated work on animal cells which culminated in Vir-
chow's system of cellular pathology. In the second half of
the 19th century, the brilliant discoveries of Louis Pasteur

and Robert Koch completely revolutionized the approach to prophylaxis and treatment of many diseases. As early as the beginning of the 19th century, the trend was to base therapeutics on the results of animal experiments and systematic observation at the bedside, and less and less on theories and speculation. Scheele's technique of isolating the active principle in crystalline form from crude drugs and medicinal plants, and Lavoisier's discoveries towards the end of the 18th century, built the foundation for a giant leap forward in chemistry in the 19th century. This coincided with the industrial revolution, and technical advances provided the medical research worker with a new set of tools which enabled him to observe more closely and analyse in great depth.

It is not possible to mention all the discoveries of important new drugs which occurred in the first half of the 19th century, but let us recall a few. In 1804 the pharmacist Friedrich Wilhelm Sertürner succeeded in isolating morphine. His success led directly to the discovery of strychnine by Pelletier and Caventou in 1818 and of quinine in 1820. So began a completely new epoch in pharmacology, in which drugs were obtained by isolating the medically active constituents from crude drugs. Charles Gabriel

Wooden pill divider.
The pill mass was rolled to the corr shape on a pill board and then divided up with scissors or a pill divider. Pill dividers were longish, toothed strips of wood or bone. They were widely used until the introduction of pill machines. Length 12½ inches.
Schweizerisches Pharmazie-historisches Museum, Basle.
Photograph: P. Heman, Basle.

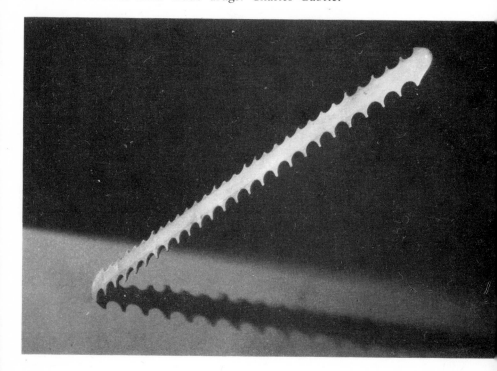

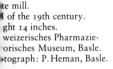

Pravaz (1791–1853) made another important therapeutic advance by introducing the concept of hypodermic injection.

Up to the middle of the 19th century, surgical anaesthesia was seldom adequate. The anaesthetics usually comprised decoctions or alcoholic extracts of crude drugs such as mandrake or opium. The analgesic action of potent alcoholic drinks was also known and used as a last resort. The introduction of effective anaesthetics made it possible to undertake types of surgery which had been quite out of the question hitherto. In 1846, the American dentist W. T. G. Morton demonstrated ether anaesthesia on a patient undergoing surgery for a tumour on his neck.

In 1847, chloroform was used for the first time instead of ether, by the gynaecologist Simpson in Edinburgh.

In 1885, the American neurologist Corning introduced conduction and spinal anaesthesia, with cocaine.

The pharmacist's laboratory became less and less able to cope with medical demands and the industrial manufacture of medicines developed during the 19th century. Many chemical and pharmaceutical factories grew from existing pharmacies. Industrial laboratories contributed to scientific research and university laboratories made major

Draft of a letter from Louis Paste[ur]
to Napoleon III.
Pasteur is seeking the support of
Napoleon III for founding a bio-
chemical laboratory.
Universitätsbibliothek, Basle.

Copie de la lettre que j'ai adressée à l'Empereur. Elle a été remise à S.M. le 6 Septembre par le Général Favé. L'Empereur a approuvé mon projet et prié le ministre, le Samedi ?, d'y donner suite. L.P.

Paris, le 5 Septembre 1867

Sire,

Nos recherches sur les fermentations et sur le rôle des organismes microscopiques ont ouvert à la Chimie physiologique des voies nouvelles dont les industries agricoles et les études médicales commencent à recueillir les fruits. Mais le champ qui reste à parcourir est immense. Mon plus grand désir serait de l'explorer avec une ardeur nouvelle, sans être à la merci de l'insuffisance des moyens matériels.

Qu'il s'agisse de rechercher par une étude scientifique patiente de la putréfaction quelques principes capables de nous guider dans la découverte des causes des maladies putrides ou contagieuses, je voudrais trouver dans les dépendances d'un laboratoire assez spacieux un emplacement où l'installation des expériences pût avoir lieu commodément et sans danger pour la santé. Comment se livrer à des recherches sur la gangrène, sur les virus, à des expériences d'inoculation, sans un local propre à recevoir des animaux morts ou vivants! La viande de boucherie est à un prix exorbitant en Europe: elle est un embarras à Buenos-Ayres. Comment soumettre à des épreuves variées, dans un laboratoire exigu et sans ressources, les procédés qui, peut-être, rendraient sa conservation et son transport faciles! La maladie dite du sang de rate fait perdre annuellement à la Beauce quatre millions de francs: il serait indispensable d'aller, pendant plusieurs années sans doute, à l'époque des grandes chaleurs, passer quelques semaines dans les environs de la ville de Chartres pour s'y livrer à de minutieuses observations.

Ces recherches et mille autres qui correspondent, dans ma pensée, au grand acte de la transformation de la matière organique après la mort et du retour obligé de tout ce qui a vécu au sol et à l'atmosphère, ne sont compatibles qu'avec l'installation d'un vaste et riche laboratoire.

Le temps est venu d'affranchir les sciences expérimentales des misères qui les entravent. Tout nous y invite : l'excitation d'un grand règne et la nécessité de maintenir la supériorité intellectuelle de la France vis à vis des efforts de nations rivales.

Sous l'inspiration de ces généreux desseins j'ai proposé à Son Excellence le ministre de l'instruction publique la fondation, sous ma direction, d'un laboratoire de chimie physiologique largement doté. En chimie animale, j'essaierais de devenir le disciple de notre grand physiologiste, Claude Bernard, que la maladie arrête momentanément au milieu de ses triomphes. En chimie végétale, je poursuivrais la voie ouverte par mes travaux personnels.

J'ose espérer, Sire, que Votre Majesté daignera approuver mon projet. Il serait digne d'inaugurer la nouvelle ère de prospérité qu'Elle réserve à l'enseignement supérieur et au progrès des sciences et de leurs applications.

Je suis, avec le plus profond respect,

Sire,

De Votre Majesté

le très humble très obéissant et très fidèle serviteur

L. Pasteur

membre de l'Académie des Sciences

Medicine jar: decalcomania using
the *verre églomisé* technique.
Circa 1800.
Height 4½ inches.
Collection of Dr. E. Müller,
Beromünster.
Photograph: P. Heman, Basle.

Ship's medicine chest.
Mahogany case, hinged lid, tall
rectangular shape with handles at
the sides, with compartments for t
phials. A hinged door on the front
opens to reveal compartments with
four small tin boxes and a drawer.
English, beginning of the 19th
century.
Height 12 inches; breadth 7 inches
depth 5½ inches.
Kunsthaus Lempertz, Cologne.

contributions to progress in pure science. The work of the chemist Justus von Liebig (1803–1873) set the standards for academic research. At the age of 21, Liebig was appointed Professor of Chemistry at the University of Giessen, where he developed a unique system of teaching and research and founded Germany's first analytical laboratory. The benzene ring theory of Liebig's pupil August Kekulé von Stradonitz (1829–1896) was a corner-stone in the development of dye production from coal-tar, an industry which later formed the basis of the chemical and pharmaceutical industries. Advances in organic synthesis enabled chemists to produce new drugs. Up until the 1880's, medicines were mostly prepared from natural products, but the development of synthetic techniques vastly extended the range of drugs available.

ig's analytical laboratory in
sen.
ch by Trautschold, 1842.
sches Museum, Munich.
ograph: Lichtbildstelle,
sches Museum, Munich.

Twentieth century

So many important pharmaceutical discoveries have been made in the last seventy years that it is only possible to mention a few of the most notable. Technical advances of the 20th century have steadily widened the scope of medical research.

In 1895, Wilhelm Conrad Röntgen (1845–1923) discoverd X-rays. This proved to be of enormous diagnostic and therapeutic importance. In 1900, K. Landsteiner announced the discovery of blood groupings and this significant advance made it possible for blood to be transfused without putting the patient at risk.

The eminent scholar Paul Ehrlich (1854–1915) was the founder of modern chemotherapy. In 1909 he and S. Hata discovered salvarsan, a chemotherapeutic agent which would cure syphilis without any major side effects.

Sulphonamides were developed from work done by Ehrlich on the selective bactericidal action of certain azo dyestuffs. ‹Prontosil› (1935), developed by Domagk, was the first sulphonamide to be used therapeutically. This and later sulphonamides achieved major therapeutic prominence although, subsequently, antibiotics replaced sulphonamides for many clinical applications.

In 1867, Pasteur and Joubert reported that certain substances produced by microorganisms have an antimicrobial action of their own. The classic example of this is the Penicillium mould which produces the antibacterial agent penicillin; this was discovered and described by Fleming in 1929 and penicillin was isolated by Chain and Florey in 1940. In 1944, Waksman and his colleagues isolated streptomycin from other fungi. This compound proved to be effective against tuberculosis. Following the discovery of penicillin and streptomycin, many new antibiotics have been isolated and, as a result of this antibiotic research, much of which is complex and painstaking, many potentially dangerous infections can now be treated successfully.

Antibiotics	Year of discovery	Total synthesis
Penicillin	1929	1957
Streptomycin	1944	–
Gramicidin S	1944	1957
Bacitracin	1945	
Chloramphenicol	1947	1949
Cephalosporin	1948	1965
Chlortetracycline	1948	–
Erythromycin	1952	–
Tetracycline	1953	–
Oleandomycin	1954	–
D-Cycloserine	1955	1955
Novobiocin	1956	1962
Mitomycin	1956	–
Demethylchlortetracycline	1957	–
Anthramycin	1963	1966

Nickel case containing 12 ‹Tubu
Schweizerisches Pharmazie-
historisches Museum, Basle.
Photograph: P. Heman, Basle.

Tuberculosis used to be one of the most common infectious diseases and, following the introduction of strepto-

...efeld filter.
...esigned by Wilhelm Berkefeld
...5–1897). Inside there is a candle-
...ed filter of kieselguhr which is
...rvious to bacteria. Water and
...r liquids to be filtered are placed
...e and forced out under positive
...gative pressure.
...r 20th century.
...ht 19 inches.
...eizerisches Pharmazie-
risches Museum, Basle.
...ograph: P. Heman, Basle.

mycin, in 1952, another tuberculostatic agent, isonicotinyl-hydrazine (INH), was discovered.

Inoculation is also an important way of combating infectious diseases. In parts of Asia, the use of artificial infection is a long-established method for producing immunity against a specific disease (variolation against smallpox). In 1796, the English physician Edward Jenner (1749–1823) became the first person in Europe to vaccinate successfully against smallpox. However, the battle against many other infectious diseases was not really joined until the work and discoveries of Pasteur and Koch had been published. Today, there is a vast range of active and passive vaccines available for prophylaxis and therapy.

The concept of the hormone emerged at the beginning of the 20th century. In 1901, J. Takamine succeeded in crystallizing adrenaline, an adrenocortical hormone, and adrenaline was the first hormone to be produced synthetically. This was done by Stolz in 1904. More than thirty steroids have been isolated from the adrenal cortex, particularly productive research work in this field being done by Reichstein, Kendall, Winterstein and Pfiffner. At the Mayo Clinic, Hench observed that one of the corticosteroids (later named cortisone) exerts a clinical anti-inflammatory action. This discovery stimulated a great deal of research into this group of compounds.

In 1914, Kendall isolated thyroxine.

In 1921, Banting and Best discovered insulin and the advent of this pancreatic hormone completely altered the hitherto unfavourable prognosis in diabetes mellitus. Insulin was produced by total synthesis in the USA, Germany and China between 1963 and 1966.

Smith, Zondek and Aschheim made outstanding contributions in the field of sex hormone research. 1930 saw the production of crystalline mixtures of sex hormones. These experiments were the prelude to an important ad-

ring torsion balance.
de by August Sauter, Ebingen,
rtemberg.
rca 1920.
ight 15 inches; width of top
inches.
ffmann-La Roche AG, Grenzach,
rmany.
otograph: P. Heman, Basle.

vance in organic chemistry because they led to the discovery of steroids and a realization of the vital role they play in many aspects of physiology. Since most steroids only occur in minute quantities under natural conditions, techniques for synthesizing them are particularly important.

Steroids	Purification	Synthesis
Oestradiol	1933	1948
Progesterone	1934	1951
Testosterone	1935	1951
Cortisol	1937	1951
Corticosterone	1937	1951
Aldosterone	1953	1957
Prostaglandins	1957	1966

The discovery of vitamins had the effect of greatly improving the general state of health of many communities. Small quantities of these vital substances occur naturally in food and there may be a serious deterioration of general health if they are absent from the diet.

Between 1907 and 1910, Funk and Holst demonstrated experimentally that scurvy is due to avitaminosis. Funk, who, in 1911, succeeded in producing an extract of rice bran which was effective against beriberi, coined the term 'vitamin'. The antiberiberi factor was styled vitamin B, although today it is called the vitamin B complex, the most important substances of this complex being thiamine (B_1), riboflavine (B_2), pyridoxine (B_6), nicotinamide, folic acid and cyanocobalamine (B_{12}).

In 1928, Szent-Györgyi isolated a substance which was identical to vitamin C, and Reichstein succeeded in synthesizing vitamin C in 1933. Kuhn and Morris synthesized vitamin A in 1937.

The following table shows the year of synthesis of some of the vitamins:

C	1933	E	1938
B₂	1935	B₆	1939
B₁	1936	Folic acid	1946
A	1937	D	1959

The discovery and exploitation of alkaloids had a profound effect on drug research. The German pharmacist Sertürner isolated the first alkaloid, morphine, from opium in 1804. Isolation of codeine and papaverine followed later. Morphinans, derived from morphine, are used as analgesics and cough suppressants.

Ergot alkaloids have a sympatholytic action and induce uterine contraction. Systematic investigation of the effects of ergot carried out by Dale and Barger led to the isolation of ergotoxine and ergotinine (1906). The major toxic constituents of ergot are the secale alkaloids which are derivatives of lysergic acid. Other representatives of this group include ergotamine, isolated by Stoll in 1918, and ergometrine. Synthetic derivatives of lysergic acid are among

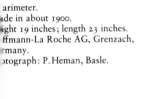

arimeter.
de in about 1900.
ght 19 inches; length 23 inches.
ffmann-La Roche AG, Grenzach,
rmany.
otograph: P. Heman, Basle.

the most effective agents known for treating certain forms of migraine. LSD, a potent hallucinogen, is also a lysergic acid analogue. Certain pharmacologically active constituents of ergot played an important part in the discovery of a number of other drugs. One of these was histamine, first isolated by Dale and Barger. This discovery greatly improved our understanding of allergic conditions, and Bovet's discovery of histamine antagonists in 1938 was the prelude to a whole new range of drugs, the antihistamines.

New classes of antihypertensive agents and psychotropic drugs were discovered as a result of investigations into a group of compounds derived from reserpine, a rauwolfia alkaloid.

Alkaloids derived from Indian arrow poisons, known as curare, are used as muscle relaxants in surgery. In 1940, a naturally occurring curare alkaloid, tubocurarine, was introduced as an adjunct to anaesthetics. Toxiferine was produced semi-synthetically in 1958.

Cocaine, the alkaloid from coca leaves, and derivatives of cocaine are used as local anaesthetics.

Ipecacuanha root contains a number of alkaloids and one of these, emetine, is used in amoebic dysentery.

The Citadel of Drugs.
Depicting the development of drug production from the mediaeval pharmacy up to the modern pharmaceutical industry.
Painting by Franco Assetto.
Dated 1955.
Associazione fra Titolari di Farmac Torino.

The English physician Whitering recognized the pharmaceutical importance of digitalis at the end of the 18th century and at the beginning of the 19th century research workers attempted to isolate the active principles of the plant, but the only glycoside of therapeutic importance was digitalin, prepared by Homolle in 1844. It was not clear whether digitalis contained other glycosides. However, in 1926 Cloëtta isolated the three chemically discrete, crystalline glycosides digitoxin, gitoxin and gitalin and, as a result of this discovery, digitalis treatment became really effective. In 1933, Stoll crystallized three other cardioactive glycosides from *Digitalis lanata*, lanatosides A, B and C.

Since 1950 there have been important advances in the development of psychotropic agents, and drugs like chlorpromazine and other phenothiazines have completely revolutionized the management of mental disorders. Other compounds from related classes of chemicals are now used to treat all forms of depression. Tranquillizers and ataractic agents, including meprobamate, the benzodiazepines and other synthetic drugs, have proved of immense value in the treatment of excitation states and emotional tension, ailments which are becoming a common feature of modern life with all its stresses.

:elain vessel for acids.
:a 1900.
ght 21 inches; circumference
nches.
fmann-La Roche AG, Grenzach,
many.
tograph: P. Heman, Basle.

Up until the beginning of the 20th century, biological and chemical research was the province of the university laboratory. Today academic and industrial research laboratories operate side by side, each making their own particular contribution to progress. They should be mutually complementary, and both are absolutely essential. To put this more simply: universities are mainly devoted to fundamental research, providing the source of new ideas and principles which are then used by the pharmaceutical industry as a basis for specific research and development programmes aimed at producing new drugs. The essential ingredient for success is not where the research is done, but the ability of the research worker, whether he works on his own, or as part of a team of scientists. Doctor Ernst Kretschmer has said: 'Science is a question of character, strict discipline and renunciation, a question of honesty, unflagging persistence, integrity and an unquenchable ambition to succeed.'

nd tabletting machine.
rly 20th century.
ight 13 inches.
hweizerisches Pharmazie-
torisches Museum, Basle.
otograph: P. Heman, Basle.

Acknowledgements

Lydia Mez-Mangold

It is from no sense of duty that I offer my heartfelt thanks to everyone who has given me such kind assistance with this book.

Dr. A. Lutz, Honorary Lecturer at the University of Basle and Curator of the Schweizerisches Pharmazie-historisches Museum in Basle, not only gave me very valuable advice but also agreed to scrutinize the text critically.

I am grateful to Dr. D. A. Wittop Koning, Amsterdam, for his help with the very recent specialized literature.

H. D. Schneider, Leyden, provided the illustrations for the Ancient Egyptian period.

Dr. K. Feinstein, Basle, gave me valuable assistance in the collation of the very extensive material available on 20th-century developments.

I was allowed to select suitable items from the splendid private collections of Dr. E. Müller, Beromünster, and Dr. H. Schmid, Diessenhofen.

Experts from many museums and libraries at home and abroad unselfishly gave me the most valuable assistance.

Peter Heman, Basle, knew just how to photograph the objects chosen for the illustrations.

I was greatly encouraged by the initiative and imagination of M. Schneider and H. Zaugg of Roche.

References

BURCKHARDT, T.: *Alchemie*. Olten and Freiburg i. Br.: Walter, 1960.

CASTIGLIONI, A.: *Histoire de la médecine*. Paris: Payot, 1931.

DIEPGEN, P.: *Geschichte der Medizin*. Berlin: Walter de Gruyter, 1949.

FEDERMANN, R.: *Die königliche Kunst*. Vienna, Berlin, Stuttgart: Paul Neff, 1964.

HÄFLIGER, J. A.: *Pharmazeutische Altertumskunde*. Zürich: Druckerei zur Alten Universität, 1931.

HAMARNEH, S. K., SONNEDECKER, G.: *A Pharmaceutical View of Albucasis Al-Zahrāwi in Moorish Spain*. Leyden: E. J. Brill, 1963.

VON HOVORKA, O., KRONFELD, A.: *Vergleichende Volksmedizin*. Stuttgart: Strecker & Schröder, 1908.

JONCKHEERE, F.: *Le «préparateur des remèdes dans l'organisation de la pharmacie égyptienne»*. Deutsche Akademie der Wissenschaften zu Berlin. Institut für Orientforschung, publication No. 29. Berlin: Akademie-Verlag, 1955.

JÖRIMANN, J.: Frühmittelalterliche Rezeptarien. Thesis, Zürich, 1925.

LUTZ, A.: Die Adaption arabischer medizinischer Weisheit im hohen Mittelalter. *Schweiz. Rsch. 61*, 72 (1962).

LUTZ, A.: Das Dynameron des sogenannten Nikolaos Myrepsos und das Antidotarium Nicolai. *Veröffentl. int. Ges. Gesch. Pharm.* N.F. *21*, 57–73 (1963).

LUTZ, A.: Das *Dispensarium ad aromatarios* des Nicolaus Praepositus (correct Prepositi) um 1490 und seine Bedeutung für die Geschichte der Pharmazie. *Veröffentl. int. Ges. Gesch. Pharm.* N.F. *26*, 87–103 (1965).

MEYER-STEINEGG, T., SUDHOFF, K.: *Geschichte der Medizin im Überblick*. Jena: Gustav Fischer, 1928.

MØLLER, K. O.: *Pharmakologie*. Basle, Stuttgart: Schwabe, 1966.

MÜRI, W.: *Der Arzt im Altertum*. Extracts from Greek and Latin sources, with German translations. Munich: Heimeran, 1938.

SCHELENZ, H.: *Geschichte der Pharmazie*. Berlin: Julius Springer, 1904.

SIGERIST, H. E.: *Anfänge der Medizin*. Zürich: Europa-Verlag, 1963.

TSCHIRCH, A.: *Allgemeine Pharmakognosie*. Leipzig: B. Tauchnitz, 1933.

ndex of proper names

Figures in italics
denote mention in picture captions.

We acknowledge with thanks the contributions of the following to the production of this book:

Layout:	Hans Zaugg, Roche Graphics Department
Photolithographs:	Photolitho Sturm, Muttenz
Typesetting:	Kreis & Co. Ltd, Basle
Editing and original idea:	Martin Schneider
Translated from the German by:	T.L. and J.A.L. Janson